SO BE IT...

How I Found MYSELF
In This Crazy World

Based on the true story of a single Indian woman

LATIKA TRIPATHI

authorHOUSE®

AuthorHouse™ UK Ltd.
500 Avebury Boulevard
Central Milton Keynes, MK9 2BE
www.authorhouse.co.uk
Phone: +441908309250

This book is a work of non-fiction. Unless otherwise noted, the author
and the publisher make no explicit guarantees as to the accuracy
of the information contained in this book and in some cases, names
of people and places have been altered to protect their privacy.

First published by AuthorHouse 7/15/2009

ISBN: 978-1-4389-8552-7 (sc)

This book is printed on acid-free paper.

www.sobeitthebook.com

Photography by Harpreet Bachher
www.harpreetbachher.com

For my **Son**,

your very being has given me a purpose for being

with all my love, now and forever…

ACKNOWLEDGMENTS:

So many people have inspired this book that it would be impossible to mention them all here.

My special thanks to Dr. Newton Kondaveti, M.D. for showing me the spiritual path with unconditional love and eternal wisdom, Dr. G.V. Lakshmi, M.B.B.S. for her guidance in helping me to assimilate my past-life experiences, Mini Khurana my assistant for her unstinted support, Sudipto and Monobina Das, my family, friends and colleagues who have always stood by me.

FOREWORD:

I met this amazing woman when she attended her NLP Practitioner program and was inspired by her. She gave 100% in developing her skills and was totally going for it. During one of the breaks she shared with me that she was trying to write her life story. So I suggested she stop 'trying' and just do it. When only a couple of months later Latika asked me to read her book I was honoured and intrigued. I am a curious person curious of people and enjoy stories and metaphors... and what a treat this book is! I couldn't put it down...

I wonder why you have picked up this book. Fate? Destiny? Boredom? Curiosity? Have you ever stopped and wondered how life is different for other people compared to your own experience of it? Imagine what it would be like to grow up in a different country, in a different culture and lifestyle to anything you know? This book is an Indian woman's adventure.

This is the life story of a woman who learns the lessons of life. Some of them the hard way and others in wonderful moments of clarity. Her childhood installs her beliefs and as she grows into an adult, wife and mother she seeks to learn who she really is.

As an Expat, working and living in a foreign country, is it common to wonder about the differences of people? Deep down we are the same. Only our experiences are different. Ultimately we all have the same issues. Our story just becomes how we package it. As Latika shares her journey you can identify with your own learnings.

Latika has a great style of writing. I love her use of language, great metaphors and at times I really felt as if I was there with her, enjoying the ups and downs of her adventure. Other than those must have bathroom breaks and making a cup of coffee, I was totally captured. I could relate to more than I thought possible. After I had finished I stopped and thought about who I was being. Who am I really? What is it that I am searching for that I already have? What more will complete me? And of course – I found some answers of my own.

So as you read this book, prepare to be intrigued. You will find more of you than you think.

And if you choose to not continue, then you will be left wondering.

I am a coach. My job is to hear other people's stories about how their life isn't perfect yet. I assist them in taking action to get the life they want and deserve. I was recently talking to a book coach (or book midwife as she likes to be known as). She believes that there is a book in everyone. That got me wondering... what is my story? This author has shown me the possibility. And I wonder what yours is?

Thanks Latika – your story has inspired me to be more of me and to only seek more what will add icing to my cake. And I really like icing!

Wendy Shaw,

NLP Master Coach and Consultant,

Dubai, UAE.

Introduction:

This book is the tapestry of my life. As the master weaver, I have woven complex, unique patterns into it without a blueprint to guide me.

I have recorded the journey of my life in eight chapters, each one a colourful strand stretched between my past to my present. Each chapter has a theme that journeys alone as well as intertwines with all the others. The overlapping of strands and themes create an amazingly harmonious design of diverse colours and patterns.

Like an onion being peeled layer by layer, so does each chapter begin by addressing the outermost reality. Bit by bit, the inner contents are exposed. I didn't peel the onion perfectly, but I approached each layer with joyful anticipation. I also had to accept that tears and blurred eyes were a part of the deal.

The peeling of the many layers of the onion is the most difficult part. There certainly is joy in having the tears pour down without any shame, anyone who has peeled an onion would agree. Even though the tears sting and the eyes burn as the tears pour out, the sinuses clear up. It is the ultimate process of healing.

In crying we release. In releasing we let go. In letting go, we start accepting. In accepting we are. In being we become. In becoming we fly. In flying we see ourselves as the tiniest beings, a mere speck on this planet and the universe.

That is when we are willing to put aside our bad moments and look at the whole picture.

As we see our tapestry from a distance and notice it in its entirety for the first time, we see that it has a unique pattern to it. The patterns are familiar too. It is the beautiful design of our life and very dear to us. All parts of it. Even the parts where the design was woven wrong.

The good, the bad, and the ugly. The happy moments are appreciated more because we have known what sad is. The giving and the receiving. The joy of finding your love and the sorrows of having lost your loved ones. The wows and the hows. The yes has more meaning because of the previous no. The complete picture. At a glance. We don't have to rework the strands, we get the ability to see it all at once in all the hues and get all the insights at one go. When you reach the core, everything is heightened. Even the silence has definite sound to it.

Then everything else ceases to matter and we are able to live in the now. We finally accept. With unconditional love, to anything that has been or will be we can simply say, SO BE IT.

Chapter 1:

Being

Who we are is primarily defined for us by our caregivers and parents. Despite the best of intentions, they sometimes get it wrong. In my opinion, aspiring parents to be should be put through compulsory counselling together to ensure they realize and agree on what parenting entails before they create a new life.

In earlier times, children had more siblings, and parents enjoyed the support of extended family nearby. Problems were solved with the input of uncles, aunts, and grandparents, and even sibling rivalry helped to give a clearer sense of identity. In odd cases of incompetent parenting, a child could look up to a better role model within the family.

In these days of nuclear families and single parenting, it is imperative to prepare for this role with utmost caution. It would be a safer and better world if we made our children our priority. Most certainly we would not see so many kids go astray in these disturbed times with its overexposure to everything. In this imperfect world, we often have kids first and realize the gravity of what we have done later.

This chapter talks about my identity crisis and how I learnt from it. I am trapped in it even today. Some skins are not so easy to shed.

———

It was a deep and dark December in a small Indian town called Dehradun, close to the Ganges and far away from any major city. A smiling, crying bundle of joy arrived to her proud parents. They rejoiced at the first child that they had been blessed with. They counted the fingers and the toes of the plump, healthy baby and were full of gratitude. They promised to take good care of this perfect creation. They didn't know then that some promises made are impossible to keep. The next decades would try them and the baby in every way possible. This is the story of that child.

I was born a Brahmin[1] girl in a typically vegetarian, non-drinking, non-smoking, non-violent, and extremely religious extended family of farmers.

My dad nicknamed me 'Beta', which translates to 'son'. It was his way of feeling he had a son, when he really only had two daughters. He hardly ever called me by my real name, and he never realized that that word made me more of a man than any other experience in my life. My identity crisis started then.

I was gifted with *The Ugly Duckling* storybook when I was seven, and it only added to my confusion. I went about my entire life thinking that that was me. I did sometimes believe that the ugly duckling would one day grow into a beautiful swan, but that idea was usually forgotten amidst the many challenges life presented. The addition of braces to my protruding teeth at age twelve only intensified these feelings.

———

1 *Hindu priestly class.*

My dad, who had chosen to be an officer in the Indian Army and move away from his farming future, had suffered when he was forced to change his habits entirely and live the typical Armed Forces lifestyle. As part of his training, he had to learn to subsist on things like quail, partridges, and sometimes snakes. As children, my sister and I grew up eating practically everything, so that a day should not come when we would have to suffer and be forced to adjust our diets. So the Brahmin girls went about life eating mutton do pyaza and chicken biryani and relishing the partridge pickle and other delicacies unheard of in our farmer uncles' lives.

Westernized to the hilt, never thinking about the Brahmanism that I was born into, I moved on, happy with whatever I saw and enjoying it all. During summer holidays when all the cousins would meet at our grandparents' house, I developed an unusual feeling of superiority over them.

They ate only vegetables and did not know that gin, which I had once accidentally imbibed from my dad's glass at lunch, looked just like water but tasted like fire. They said 'yuck' when we spoke about how mouthwateringly delicious chicken tandoori was.

I enjoyed their obvious discomfort when I showed off with tales of touching fish in the fish market or watching the blood spill from a chicken's freshly split throat. As we grew, they still didn't know any basic knowledge, like that beer makes an excellent conditioner for hair that was limp and had no body. My superiority complex crept in without anyone knowing any better.

I would fight the boys in the officers' mess while other girls my age acted shy and coy when the boys were around. I was always one of the guys and often spoke and sat and behaved like them. The boys saw me as a buddy, too, as I didn't do all those girly things. I was always part of the gang, which was good for me, but there were times when they were on the receiving end of my antics.

One incident occurred at a formal farewell dinner for an outgoing officer of the regiment. All the children were expected to stay out of sight in a room far away from the main hall where the adults partied on. It was after eleven o' clock, and all the kids were sleepy but no one would be the first to admit feeling tired. It was an unannounced competition.

At that point, my sister, who was about seven, called out to me and said she was really sleepy and wanted to lie down. The older boys, about nine and closer to my own age, snickered and called her names. My anger burst forth like a volcano erupting, and I dived onto the main culprit. Before I realized what was going on, all the other boys came to protect their gang leader and jumped on me and punched me hard. I was enraged at the injustice, but at the same time I didn't know how to pull out of the pile or what to do next; I was shocked by their unexpected ganging up against me.

In the confusion of hands and feet, between being pushed down and trying to stand up, I reached for what seemed to be a fleshy arm and bit firmly into the skin. I tightened the grip of my teeth until I felt moisture on my lips. A loud howl from the gang leader silenced the entire party, and soon the parents rushed in and pulled apart this melee of children.

The gang leader was rushed to the army nursing room, and I got the worst talking to from my mom, who admonished me to behave like a girl. I was surprisingly collected after that release of anger. I must have looked like a Halloween partier with drops of the boy's blood still beaded on the corners of my lips, but I responded to my mom very calmly that it just was not a manly thing for me to allow an outsider to tease my sister. Besides, only I had the right to torture her. The intensity with which I spoke silenced my mom as she realized that I really meant it. She was horrified, and later when she narrated this incident to anyone she always added, 'Why can't she be like the younger one, my angel?'

My dad stayed out of this even though he was present at the scene, as it was considered appropriate for mothers to handle such situations. As I lay in bed that night, my dad came and tucked the mosquito net neatly around me and whispered, 'Well done, Son. I am so proud. That was very brave of you. Don't let anyone ever treat you or your loved ones badly.'

That became my defining moment. All my life thereafter I have often dived into stuff like that and stood by the weaker party, being brave for them and never caring about the consequences. Of course I learnt that bleeding someone was not the best way to make a point.

What's wrong is wrong. The sooner this is cleared, the lesser the pain for all involved.

Often a mother and a father go about parenting each in their own unique manner and don't come to a joint agreement as to how they should raise their offspring. It was like that with my parents. They both went about it in their individual way, and neither conferred with the other. It led to a lot of confusion within me, as often I did not know which way to go.

It is important to instil core values into kids at an early age, which my parents did very well. They imparted honesty, integrity, industriousness, determination, focus, humour, and intelligence to me and my sister early on. Despite their best intentions towards me, their first born, they got it wrong in the most important area by not communicating with each other. Maybe instilling clarity into their kid didn't occur to them, or perhaps they didn't have that within them in the first place.

My identity was sealed when I bit the bully. I would be both boy and girl; I had to go on fluctuating between those two depending on the situation, I thought to myself. Was I not half the cells from my mom and half from my dad anyway? Biology came to my rescue.

That incident was the last time those boys spoke up in my presence. I was the uncrowned champion with all the girls and all the boys too, except for the bandaged gang leader. Soon after, his dad was transferred, and thankfully my bad reputation was washed away.

My sister saw me as a support through that fiasco, and whenever she was in trouble or needed advice she would come to me for an opinion; even now she continues to do that. Often my solution was to take over the matter by personally going to the person who she had a problem with and saying whatever had to be said as if she was saying it. This was no real solution at all, and I did not realize that I was becoming a bully now. After that the problem would go away and in fact the person causing the problem would never come close to either her or me. Nobody knew any better at home.

As a fee for all this free emotional protection, my sister received regular hammerings from me if she didn't comply in certain situations. She isn't joking when she says she is short because I never allowed her to grow. I would just keep banging her back into the earth at regular intervals. Physical fights amongst us were not so frequent, but there were some real lessons that I learnt through play.

One such time we were left at home while mom went out to replenish the weekly groceries. I was the mistress of the house, and my sister was to play the part of the housemaid. In this role she had to clean the kitchen and the toilets and keep the food ready in time for the master to return home. She did all her assigned tasks rather quickly and came to me, the mistress. 'Ma'am, pardon me for disturbing your siesta, but all the work is done. When will the master come home for lunch?' 'Later,' I said, 'and since all the chores are done and you have nothing else to do until the master returns, I would like you to massage my tired feet for a while.'

The 'housemaid' became aggressive and rude and said that that was not part of her job. Like any good mistress, I was outraged and would not stand such rebellion from the help. I told her to get out of the house and never come back. She started crying and apologized. After expelling my sister, I returned to the imaginary world of the privileged mistress and continued to rest her tired feet.

Everything was alright for the next hour or so until the real mistress, my mom, returned from the weekly shopping trip only to find her little daughter locked out of the house and crying like a lost orphan. My sister related the housemaid's sad tale, and I never played the mistress again after that. I graduated to playing a lot of 'doctor-doctor' in my teenage years though. When I was married and managed a home of my own, I was always careful to be friendly, rather than superior, to all my domestic help.

My mom had settled that once and for all by making me the housemaid and giving two days of leave to the paid helpers. My sister floated about the house in joy while I was made to clear and wash her plates and dishes, polish her shoes, and iron her school uniform as a final reinforcement to ensure the demon mistress never returned.

At that time not only did I have an identity crisis, but my bullying became worse, as now I would do it without my mom's knowledge. I became a bit of a liar, too. The person who has suffered the most because of my identity crisis, besides me, has been my sister.

Despite being so thin as to appear almost malnourished those days, I believed I was strong, and that often made me do things that others would have turned their head from and politely declined to participate in. Confident of winning, I went wherever the action was. My inner strength carried me through a lot of unpleasant situations in life.

Often I was expected to respond differently in situations as compared to my sister. It made me feel superior, and along with this dad would whisper to me that I was the son and could easily do it.

For example, all the banking was assigned to me at an early age while he was away on a posting to a border area. Not only did I withdraw and deposit money, but mom asked me to perform the more complex task of budgeting for the entire household. Her relationship with money was bad, or so my father revealed in one of the secret confidences he shared with me.

While kids my age were being responsible for taking the trash out or feeding the family cat, I was adding up all the expenses and setting aside money for the daily expenditures until the next payday. That's when I developed a love for numbers. I became very adept at juggling things and could find solutions to the seemingly impossible. As a child I had the advantage of not being bound by the limitations that adults feel as they often turn down the most obvious solutions.

Although this ability benefited me later in life, it put a lot of pressure on my less than fourteen-year-old mind. While I suffered and was confused in other areas, I was very confident and had perfect clarity when it came to money. Since my friends could not understand my thought process, I was often the outcast for knowing too much. The identity crisis deepened further. Was I a carefree child or a financial wiz?

That parents can harm their own flesh and blood without even realizing it, and then further compound their mistakes by not discussing them with one another, is a lesson I have learnt well and been careful not to inflict on my own child. Young people cannot be expected to take over adult roles just because parents are weak or incompetent in some areas. The terrible money handling on part of my mom placed a huge burden on me. It has helped me later but was a big weight to carry those days. My great responsibilities made me a serious person when I should have been free to be a child, making the normal mistakes that children make and learning from them.

This inappropriate financial responsibility has defined a large part of me. Many things I do have to be completed perfectly, leaving no room for error, and no room for much else either. Spontaneity was totally missing from my life, and only recently have I reclaimed it.

Around age fourteen, I could no longer pretend to be a son, so I developed a kind of convenient split where I would be the Beta when my dad was around and play the 'swan', which I was now beginning to enjoy, when he wasn't. That was the beginning of a long and dangerous ride.

My mom tried in vain to make a girl of me. My sister was the delicate one and I was the wild one. To please my mother I took to knitting and cooking, and I even became very good at stitching clothes. I was the perfect son to dad and the almost perfect daughter to my mom, who was impossible to please. My sister was always the perfect daughter and continues to be.

Mom was just trying to get all the chores done, since dad was away often. She never reinforced tenderness and love with her children. Discipline and good manners were her theme. Any physical display of affection was rare.

I saw my friends being hugged and kissed frequently by their parents, and it seemed strange to me that people would do that so often to each other and for apparently no reason at all. It wasn't even their birthday, I marvelled when I was younger; it wasn't as if they had performed exceptionally well at school or at a sport, I reasoned when older. I was unable to understand why other families made such a big deal of it.

While spending a day at a girlfriend's house, I watched her rush out of the room to hug and greet her dad when he returned from work. When I asked her why she had just done that, she replied that she always did when he came home. Always? Every day? I wondered. When I asked mom why we didn't hug every day, she had no answer and neither did that motivate her to consider becoming more expressive. I found getting myself more and more confused, as we just did not express our feelings so openly despite obviously loving each other.

We were really good at expressing our anger or sharing our feelings or thoughts, minus the physical hugs and kisses and the actual words 'I love you'. Everything else was discussed. Nothing negative was ever kept hidden, waiting to surface at some inopportune moment. There was never any negativity left to deal with later. Everything was handled swiftly and immediately. We got really good at releasing all our feelings. A part of me enjoyed this process of releasing as any boy would. Sometimes our love was expressed through anger, too. It seems odd, but in our family we knew that this anger was an expression of love and not real animosity.

Between ages fourteen and sixteen, all was well with me. Suddenly I was the swan. I knew it and capitalized on it big time. The dating started, and I went out with a continuous string of boys, many wilder than me. After all the years I plagued my mom, it was now my boyfriends' turn to deal with me and unsuccessfully try to make a girl out of me.

They had a tough time. I was too much of a guy, but they figured that out only later. What they expected and were used to was a typical Indian girlfriend, soft-spoken, pretty, delicate, demure, blushing, coy, giggling perhaps, and ditzy. She would cry easily, and then it was up to the boyfriend to patch things up and buy her gifts and chocolates or roses.

I was extremely deceptive in this area. I certainly looked the part during the first two dates. I was extremely adept at shifting gears between the boy–girl personas by now. But by and large the masculine aspect surfaced at the third date, and the unsuspecting boyfriend would be rather amused at my occasional swearing. From meeting number four onwards, my boyishness would dominate, and I'd remain a complete tomboy until the end of the relationship.

Sometimes I would let out a string of words that would make the boys blush for me. When they said something out of line I would smack them on their arms or back. As our familiarity grew, I graduated to slapping them on the face. They were too shocked to react. I once hit one of them where it hurts the most, and he doubled up on the floor in pain and squeaked out what sounded like nasty words. Even today I have no idea what they were, as he wasn't at his eloquent best then. He wouldn't repeat them to me when I told him later that I didn't quite catch what he said while he was curled up on the floor; perhaps he was afraid of a repeat treatment. He had to wheel his motorbike home, as he wasn't able to sit very well. His rather tight jeans didn't help either. We broke up soon after.

Word spread. Many such instances made me hot property amongst all the boys between sixteen, my own age, and twenty-one. My reputation grew, and each wanted to try his luck, confident that he would emerge the champion. Taming of the shrew could have been their theme. No one ever won with me. I would always come out on top. Winning was in me. Whether it was love or war, I didn't differentiate. Very rarely I would let one of them feel good by letting the fight end in a good round of animal sex. Indirectly, he would think he had won that round. It only happened when I liked that one particularly more than anyone else.

Extremely critical of whom I was seeing and always warning us of the possible consequences, mom became the enemy. I learnt to block her out completely. I could handle myself.

I decided I was going to take charge of my life as soon as possible. Studying doubly hard and determined to move away from the family as soon as possible I graduated in commerce and obtained a hotel management diploma at the same time. Additionally, I studied German just in case I got a job as a translator and got an opportunity to move to Germany, which was one of the places I had always wanted to visit when I grew up. My choice of language also gravitated towards the more guttural and manly one as compared to the delicate French that most of my peers opted for in college.

Finally, and it couldn't have been soon enough for me, I started out in Bombay. A job with a leading hotel helped me finance my stay in this city of dreams.

Still going about life as either a boy or a girl depending on the situation I was in, I found Bombay accepted me in no time at all. I felt that the city had been waiting for me to come and discover it.

I smoked now and drank and led a pretty active social life, hitting all the night spots and living the life of a twentysomething. To be seen as someone who was game for anything and with very little inhibitions and no parents around made it that much easier. There was a lot to see, and I learned the ropes quickly.

I realized later I attracted men in my life who were extremely expressive with their emotions, because that was what I never got when I was younger and what I deeply craved. The identity crisis and its deeper questions were never really answered at all. After a while I got heavily involved with dating, which resulted in a quick marriage to a colleague who was many years older. That made him a good choice for the wild and reckless me. I had barely known him for six months before I agreed to the marriage. He had proposed within a month of my joining this leading publication house. I never did pursue the hotel job. In retrospect, it was my not knowing what I really wanted that made me vulnerable to his insistence to get married and live in a home of our own in Bombay instead of boarding in a working women's hostel.

He won only because I didn't know my mind and heart or even myself; I figured that if someone was so crazy about me, how could he possibly be an unsuitable partner. My outer confidence made people believe that I really was sure of myself, but inside I was just a lost and wide-eyed mix of boy–girl.

After that, I was really caught up with my home, child, and career. The question of identity now revolved around my roles as wife, mother, successful manager, or youngest chairperson of the housing complex where we lived.

I purchased a house against strong opposition from my husband, who thought it wasn't a good idea to look for financing from a bank. I went into it alone, and at some point he was convinced that owning was better than paying rent. I could be stubborn about things I really wanted. I made most of the difficult, and usually male, decisions the entire time I was married, even the decision to get divorced.

During my nine years of marriage, I still did not know who I was. I was a bit of everything I was expected to be, and on my own I was nothing. I defined myself based on who I was with and never thought of who I was when I was alone.

At that time it didn't matter, because I had not been alone for long periods of time. Everything was just happening to me, as opposed to my being responsible for creating anything at all. Life was a series of accidents back then, many good ones and some nasty ones. No single situation ever had me worried for long periods of time.

It got to a point where I was looking to find quick solutions to every challenge, to keep all parties happy. I always had all the answers and often thought that life was just a big game to be played and won, always easily excelling. And I did.

I never questioned until I was hit with thunder and lightning from the skies and was stripped of all the layers of conditioning wrapped around me. The cocoon within which I had become so comfortable was forcibly peeled off, and I was exposed to the strongest sunlight and blinded. All I could do was grope around.

This was when my identity was finally challenged and threatened.

I was already confused, and there was more and more being dumped on me. As the stark reality hit me, I was forced to choose to continue to live with my husband, whom I was told was cheating on me even though he was the one who had chased me to get married to him nine years ago, or to opt out of the marriage and live alone with my son. Armed with the information I was given, I gave my husband the ultimatum to choose the other person or me, and to my shock he chose to move out.

This was a blessing in disguise, as he didn't try to fight for the custody of my son, my only anchor and reason to go on. We spent our last night under the same roof on 1 May 2000.

I was now totally alone in Bombay with no dad to fall back on, no husband, and no savings. The life of a single parent of a five-year-old, lost in the sea of people and the fast pace of life in Bombay, would challenge anyone, especially someone who still had no idea of her very identity. I thought I was sinking, being pulled down and thrashed about by the shark from *Jaws*. How could it be? I could not lose. I always had been the winner.

I turned to mom, who came to my rescue in a flash. She took over my daily troubles of managing my less than five year old son and the house at a time when I could not even get myself to get into the shower each morning.

There was nothing to look forward to now. Mom could not help in any other way. All she could tell me was to pray. I could never relate to her, and as usual whatever she said fell on deaf ears. My confidence was completely shattered. I was dead on the inside and would have very well jumped into a well or from the top of a tall tower, as my life had very little purpose then.

The only thing that prevented me was the thought of leaving my son alone in this world alone for no fault of his own. That was my only thread to sanity, and even then it kept me sane for brief periods only. Later I learnt to utilize both the masculine and feminine sides of myself to give this boy both the parents rolled into one. This was the one way my split identity actually worked well for me, I think.

I turned to my sister too. She stood by me like a rock and offered unconditional emotional and financial assistance. She was the silent strength behind me. But all her support and all the love she showered on me and her nephew could not help me to understand who I was - the basic thing I needed to know before I could move to the next set of life questions I wanted to solve.

My sincere search for my identity began then, at age thirty and alone. In the nine years since, I think I have found the answer. I did what I have always done when in doubt, jump in a la Superman. Choosing to go ahead with the divorce, I started life afresh with my son and thought I would handle the identity issue later on, when I had the luxury of time.

I tricked myself into believing things would magically fall into place if only I could find that key that would open all the doors and locate the right door that would give me a happily ever after life. I changed my name twice to get the right vibrations to achieve that.

In numerology I discovered instant success and a sense of everything falling in place, only to later realize that while it gave in some areas, it took away in some other very critical areas. The name change hadn't been done correctly the first time around, and I learnt this the hard way.

It became a joke when I announced to my colleagues one Monday morning that I had changed my name over the weekend and was to be addressed by the new name. They thought it was a silly prank. No one believed me. To get them to take me seriously, I had to stop answering to the earlier name and only respond when people addressed me by my new name.

They all wanted to know what had brought this about. I had bumped into this young man who was visiting my house along with a feng shui consultant. While I was busy getting the directions sorted out with the consultant, this youthful numerologist sat in my living room and worked on my name. He asked me for my date of birth and went about doing some quick calculations.

He explained that numerology is the science of getting the name aligned to the date of birth to ensure that they are in harmony. It's all about the vibrations that we send out, and if the vibrations of our name are not in sync with our date of birth, things keep going wrong in our lives despite our best efforts. That is what was happening to me, he explained.

What were the chances I would not buy that? The numerologist suggested a change in the spelling of my existing name. I didn't like that option of double 'k's and 't's, so I went about picking a new name. My identity crisis made me gladly accept this as the solution to all my so far unsuccessful attempts to find my real self. I would take on a new avatar and fool the old identity with this new me. He suggested this perfect name numerologically, and I went along with it.

Two years later, it turned out that the number he had so confidently recommended was faulty. First, there were the unending procedures that I had gone through to legally change my name. Then followed the troubles that the faulty name number landed me in.

Getting deeper into the mess, I realized that I would have to take the matter in my own hands, and I began to study numerology. With little trust of anyone else, I decided to get the right calculations. My previous love for numbers came right to my rescue. I explored numerology until I had educated myself in both the Western and the Indian methods.

I changed my name for the second time. This time it was like magic. Absolutely perfect. Things fell in place into my giant jigsaw puzzle with ease, but something was still missing. A strange feeling of incompleteness came over me. Slowly the reality hit that it's more than just adding up to the right number. It's not the vibrations you put out but the vibrations you have within that matter.

I saw Shakespeare's quote 'What's in a name?' in a different light now. He was a wise soul. 'What's in your name?' he would have asked me for sure. If only this rose knew that it was the smell that defined me and not my name, I would not have gone and worked on that earlier. As I said, I was not clear then or for a long time later on.

Without any idea or a sense of knowing what I was looking for, I intensified the search and went round and round until I felt I was chasing my own tail. I figured that there are five senses, so if it is not the sound of the name, then perhaps it is in the smell that one puts out. Perhaps I was sending out a smell of fear or loneliness? And if not that, then we are left with touching. All I touched turned to gold easily. Seeing was next, and I did see it all when I travelled from one county to another. Finally it rested on the tasting. Success tasted sweet but just ever so briefly. One by one I realized that the answer was not in any of these senses.

The search and comparisons had just started. After two name changes, a divorce that took two long years to finalize, and a son sent away to boarding school, I moved to Dubai. The roads there challenged me to break all the speed limits as I zipped about the lanes with the roof of my car pulled down and my hair blowing in the hot desert breeze. My music threatened to deafen the seemingly soundproofed city. Dubai was heaven.

I drove the car of my dreams, successfully managed a career that got me a double promotion and double the salary in record time, and then brought my son back to his home – a happy home now.

I travelled the world and started living my life in a city that fulfils dreams. With each step up the ladder of success came the saddening realization that it was not enough, and I was still searching for the elusive answer to the defining question.

We do a lot of things which we think are the right things at the time. Later I realized that I was trying to be someone else. The name change just happened to be one of those things I used to become another person. All along it was my inside self that was calling out to be looked at, while I kept looking outside.

Despite having it all only seven years after I lost it all, I still felt something was amiss. Maybe I was looking in the wrong places. I wondered if those who guided me to act in these directions knew any better themselves. If they did would they have pointed me there?

If I had had a better grounding into myself right from childhood, I would have known better than to seek their advice. Having never received formal religious grounding, I was helplessly floating around and had nothing to anchor into. I was drifting. I was lost. Only I could save myself, and I had no clue where I was supposed to start.

I had read somewhere that we are all born complete and spend our entire lives in search for this elusive thing that we think we lack, while all along it lies within us. What is this thing that I lack, I wondered.

I reviewed my entire life in reverse order trying to understand where things had gone wrong. I lacked for nothing materially. In fact I had always had it all, and easily. I gave up looking backwards in time. Ironically, it was in the regressing that I finally made some progress many years later.

Then I went through my entire life, starting at the beginning to understand when things first started going wrong. I gave this up even faster. It is the conditioning around us which makes us believe and operate from the feeling that we lack something. Then we start looking for that thing which we think we lack, and the comparison and the search begins.

Lost, confused, and tired, I gave up trying to understand. I thought that if I could just get through each day, one by one, soon enough the responsibilities would be over and then I could really look for the answer.

I'd had my plate full of stuff for so long that I had to call for a side plate to pile aside some of the things to be chewed upon later. By the simple process of elimination I had finally figured what wouldn't work for me. I didn't know if it would work later, but I had a fair sense that it would not work right then, and so that would get dumped onto the side plate.

But there is so much in the universe, and I could not possibly sample everything and every experience in life. I kept piling my side plate with stuff to be handled later. It became precariously full and overloaded and things started spilling onto the table, especially my emotions. I was becoming cold and had started to deep freeze my feelings as much as I could. Now the freezer was full too.

It hit me that the answer had to be found right away. I could not wait another day, and certainly not until the right moment came along. Is there such a thing as the right moment anyway?

They say when the disciple is ready the master appears, and just like that as I was flipping through a children's magazine, it happened. As I waited at the dentist's for my son, I read the story that changed me forever.

The story was about a lion cub raised by sheep. When the cub wandered away from the herd, he was captured by an old lion. The old lion was surprised that the cub was not able to roar and chase smaller creatures like other cubs his age enjoyed doing, but behaved and made sounds like sheep. The old lion took this cub to the lake and made him see his reflection in the still waters. When the cub saw who he really was, he let out the loudest roar ever heard from any lion cub. He had suppressed his true personality because of the conditioning he had received from the herd. He could now move around the rest of his life freely and be happy with his identity as a lion.

That hour in the dentist's reception propelled me to finding my true self. I knew then that I was holding onto the end of a thread that would unravel the more important higher truths to me. My being would be defined now. Whatever happens I should not let go of this awareness, I decided.

It is social conditioning that makes us behave differently from our true nature when we are forced to be sheep and follow the herd. The true lion lies within, and it is up to us to awaken the sleeping lion and lead the way. Nature is perfect in whatever it does. There is no room for error as far as nature is concerned. It is we humans who like to complicate things and believe that what we are creating is a correction to nature's errors. If we were meant to be clones, we would have all been born the same naturally. Some of us are meant to be different, and we are born as such. If we have the courage to recognize the lion within, then lions we all shall be.

Look at your reflection in the mirror, and see what you have believed about yourself because others conditioned you in that way.

Being a lion requires you to move alone often, to find your path and to be prepared to face the uneven territory that is part of life. By being the lions that we are meant to be, we learn the true lessons of life.

The lion goes for the kill. But his killing for food is an integral part of the cycle that nature intended. Lions have the power to protect themselves and their cubs in times of danger. Sheep may offer protection in crowds for a short time, but if faced with danger they will all cuddle and huddle away, leaving one of them alone in the face of danger.

We come alone and go alone, and that is the undeniable truth of life. Why should we be afraid to find our way alone between the coming and the going? We come from nothing and go into nothing, so why is being nothing in between not OK?

I now understand a few things better than I did in that moment three years ago. It is the sense of inner knowing and inner being that defines us, not the five senses of sound, touch, sight, taste and smell. I know now what I would like to be and where I would like to go. The journey has started and I know I'll get there.

I am still to figure out how to get there, but that is something to be figured out just as all lions have to figure it out, by being in the wild.

The most important question of them all is one that got answered for me recently – the question of who I am. The lion within says, 'I am the lighthouse that sends out beams in all directions and shows the way to others who may be on the same search of trying to understand their being just as I have been.' You can join me in this search of finding your inner lion and roar and purr as may fit the occasion.

—

Life is a series of chapters that we have to first learn and then unlearn in order to arrive at the end as we did at the beginning, pure and clean and full of faith and trust and love. In each ending there is a beginning. New starts from exactly the point where the old concludes.

CHAPTER 2:

Comparing

When you don't know who you are, you tend to compare yourself to others to try to find out if they know who they are, and then compare where you are in relation to their position.

Because I compared myself with my cousins, who were not exposed to as much life experience as my sister and I, a feeling of superiority came to me at a young age.

Later, when I compared myself with college friends who seemed to have it all, a feeling of deep inferiority came over me.

When all other comparisons were done, and all that was left to do was to compare myself to myself, the wheels started turning in the right direction. The night is darkest just before dawn, but not everybody knows that. I didn't always understand it either.

—

Being born into the culture of the Armed Forces is pretty much like being introduced to the best of life from day one. These people know how to live the lifestyles of the rich and famous. Except for their meagre salaries, nothing is small in their world.

My family moved around every two to three years, and I had attended many different schools across the country by the time I was in grade five. Making new friends came easily, and I especially loved the excitement of moving from one city to another, the packing up and unpacking and starting all over again. These multiple moves also made us adept at handling new situations.

I happily adapted a new persona with every move. I took on a new, different, more exciting identity in each city that my dad was posted to. There were always lots of stories to tell wherever we went, many of them true and some made up.

The frequency of army social functions ensured there was never a dull moment in our lives. There were plenty of outdoor activities organized by the regiment to keep the families entertained, and we had memberships to clubs for sports and swimming. Watching a movie at the outdoor cinemas was just a routine activity to us. Spending an evening out at the officers' mess with other families was a weekly affair – literally, in some cases, as many of the married women dallied with other officers, I learnt as I grew older.

The exciting events were the ones that stand out in my memory even today, such as the time we visited the underground bunkers on the border of India and Pakistan. I recall the excitement I felt as an eleven-year-old, having to bend and crouch to go deep into the earth. With each step I felt more and more like Alice in Wonderland. Lanterns kept the place barely lit. It was stuffy even for the few minutes one spent there.

Below we met the men who guarded the country around the clock. They saluted my dad from their crouched positions, seated on beds made of hardened mud. Their large rifles were fully loaded with bullets and pointed out of the tiny peepholes. When I looked through the eyepiece of the rifle, I found myself staring straight into the eyes of a Pakistani person looking right back at me. Blinking was not an option, I instinctively knew. It was the most intense moment of my life, and now I realized how important my dad's job was. He was such a noble man, ready to give up his life to protect the country. He became my hero.

We came out of the bunker and looked around at the vast land across the border. A lush green valley separated the nations, and dad explained that the piece of land between the two countries is called no-man's-land. I was stunned. It was the most beautiful piece of land I had ever seen. Someone might have really enjoyed picnicking, hiking, or camping there, but it was not possible that this was neither India nor Pakistan. It was so ironic that the birds from either side could fly freely and sit in this territory and then fly to whichever side they desired. They didn't know geography.

Over this no-man's-land was a rickety bridge much like the one I saw recently in Sri Lanka which had been left behind after the making of the movie *The Bridge Over The River Quai*. This bridge, merely wooden planks strung together with rope, was used to exchange letters twice a day when one person from each side met in the middle of the bridge. Both held a white flag to clearly signal their intentions for a peaceful meeting to exchange mail.

I saw that happen with disbelief. Could not one of them just cheat and shoot the other while face to face? No, they could not. They only shot when they had orders to, my dad clarified, when we are at war with them. And anyway they walked the bridge with just the flag in one hand and the bag of letters in the other. I was incredulous that they would only exchange the mail and return to their side safely. I observed carefully and with growing nervousness as I saw the two men come to the centre of the bridge and stop to exchange the letters. A gun or knife was hidden in their socks, I suspected. I imagined a bloody attack any minute now and saw one man hanging for his life from the rickety bridge in my mind's eye.

Suddenly the binoculars in my hand shook as the men did the most unbelievable thing: they exchanged words. How could it be? They were enemies! I was horrified. I thought my dad, the officer in charge for that post at that time, would simply sack this man on the spot for conferring with the enemy. He did not. In fact, he whispered a few questions to the man and nodded in reply. Soon my dad and I were seated in the jeep and we were off. The inspection was over.

Later, I asked my dad what the conversation had been about. He said that the Pakistani soldier's daughter had been ill the entire night. The soldier was coming down with the fever as well, and he had had to drag himself be on duty that day. I was really unable to process this information. Did they discuss families and health also? Wasn't it dangerous to tell your enemy that you had a daughter or that you were about to fall sick? Wouldn't that give the other side an upper hand? My dad explained that the countries were enemies for political reasons, but that had nothing to do with the individuals at a personal level. The Pakistani soldier was as much a human being with a daughter as my dad was.

This gave me a higher perspective of things. I have often found myself adopting this attitude. When people were unprofessional in a certain deal, I was able to keep the business and the personal sides separate, understanding that we have to do things sometimes to serve somebody else's purpose, but it need not get personal.

Obviously, I took the enmity of the countries very personally then. It was my first encounter, so I can be excused for the confusion I felt.

Contrast this adventure to a time when we were in the village during the summer holidays. Our cousins refused to go out and join a group of children who played seven tiles in the street just outside their house. I didn't know those kids, but I dragged my cousin to come out with me and join them in the game. My cousin vehemently refused to join in. I was told by him that we didn't talk to our enemies. I wondered who the enemy was. He explained to me that my lawyer uncle, his dad was fighting a case in the court against the father of one of the boys. The man had told his kids to stay away from my cousins, who also happened to be their neighbours. The boy was the leader of the group that played outside.

Even as a child, I thought that attitude was so childish. When we Indians could talk to Pakistanis about their general well-being even though the countries continued to fight, what was this enmity all about? What about neighbourly feelings?

I went out and joined the group, and we played with each other every day without my cousins until it was time for my family to return to the city. This further made me believe that it is the exposure to situations in life that truly help us to become more rounded people.

I realized another valuable lesson from this experience when I was a little older and able to process it further. In giving our kids exposure to life, we have to prepare them first so that they know what to expect and what lesson they may gain from it. We should take them only if they really will find the event of value. Otherwise parents shouldn't do it.

Many parents cart children along without letting them in on the surprising and exciting things they may encounter. Even though this method can give an adrenalin rush, it causes immense confusion.

I have tried to keep that lesson in mind, always explaining situations to my son in advance. Some of my friends who have experienced similar adventures which led to immense confusion agree with me on this.

There was a divorced mom who introduced her nine-year-old daughter to her new husband as a surprise. The child is a good friend of mine, and even in her early forties has never gotten over the shock, nor has she forgiven her mom and her poor stepfather, who still cannot understand why she does not like him.

What's normal or good news in the parents' model of the world is shocking in the child's model of world. Total surprise is not good for children below twelve years, unless it is a birthday party which they are not expecting because the dog died recently.

My family went about life doing these fantastic things. For a long time after this incident I made up spy stories and narrated them to my cousins, who had no understanding of our nomadic lives. I was wise enough to not try these fantasies out on the other army kids, who were a bunch of smarty-pants in their own way.

I think this choice of adventure was also my dad's way of ensuring he made me into a 'man'. He was born into a family of nine siblings, with seven boys and two girls. In the typical North Indian, Hindu set up that they are from girls don't count and often my grandparents would say they had seven sons and completely neglect to mention their two daughters.

As a child, I recall correcting my grandmother when she insisted on telling everyone she had seven sons. I would interrupt with 'What about your two daughters?' thinking she had forgotten about them since she had so many kids. I rationalized to myself that my grandmother's illiteracy prevented her from keeping an accurate count.

She whispered '*They* don't count.' I whispered back '*Why* don't they count?' thinking she would say that it was because they had murdered someone in the fields, but she never did answer that one.

Much later I realized my dad's need to treat me as a boy arose from the fact that he was the only one amongst his brothers who didn't have at least one son. An Indian family that lacked the important male child was incomplete, so basically my sister and I didn't count. He also called me Beta much more in the presence of his brothers, I noticed.

Another thing that I regarded as really strange and boring about our cousins' lives, besides their low exposure to life's novelty, was that they always studied. Even during the two long months of summer holidays, they were made to sit down and study for two hours every morning and at least an hour in the evenings.

I always wondered what there was to study when they had already passed the previous grade and had not even started the next class. 'Revision,' they said. 'Revision for what purpose?' I questioned. No satisfactory response ever arrived.

They smartened up over the years and somehow convinced their parents with our theory that if the grade was over, why would they need to study that same syllabus again? Couldn't they be left to enjoy the holidays just as my sister and I did, narrating stories on the veranda, making houses from matchboxes, stitching clothes for the dolls, or cooking custard or jelly?

Mom hated the holidays but encouraged us to use the imaginative part of our brains.

Our aunts and uncles would pretend to let our cousins off studying but made them read the *Encyclopaedia Britannica* or the *Ramayana* instead. My cousins are extremely smart people, and they know all the theories from the books they were forced to pour over. I have my own theories too, many based on practical experience and very few having much to do with books.

I believe that there are many ways of learning the lessons of life. Of course studying is important, but to serve what purpose? It is not an end it itself. Life is for learning. No lesson can be learnt better than through personal experience.

Oddly I was always an ace student because of my need to excel and never be second to anyone. I focused really well when in class and then studied a day or two before the exams, and that was enough to keep me in the top of the class.

I found my real education in seeing important people like the late Prime Minister Indira Gandhi, who waved out to me from her car, and meeting someone who had climbed the K2 Himalayan peak. I learned much by hearing stories of and eventually meeting the Nepalese man who had killed a tiger in his village with nothing but his bare hands and a kukri[2]. He has scars all over his face and body to show for it.

I also benefited from hearing about my dad's many adventures. Once he woke up in a sleeping bag surrounded by a six-foot snake who was apparently waiting for him to rouse.

In the 1971 war my dad got shot in his right thigh. His Nepalese batman pushed him into the trench to save his life. The batman put himself in the line of fire and was killed before he could jump in the trench too. He gave up his life for my dad.

For years after that my dad used to send money for the education of the batman's child in Nepal. I kept the accounts and was so proud of my dad. From these stories I learned to do the honourable thing. Even as the man died in my father's arms, my dad narrated later, the batman explained how he had spent the money that my dad had given to him for supplies.

I really liked that ending. I visualized myself dying and giving the accounts to my mom, who would not have understood them anyway.

---

2 *curved Nepalese knife used as both a tool and a weapon.*

When I think back today, I cannot believe such bizarre stuff happened in a battlefield. When I narrated this story to my son at age eleven or so, he would not believe it. 'It just can't be,' he said to me very confidently. I am sure he would have googled to find out if such stuff ever happened as well. Kids these days have no fun.

Sleepovers, not a concept explored in my cousins' lives, were another area of education when we spent a night at a girlfriend's place whose older brother I had a crush on. Seeing him pass by her bedroom in his pyjamas was the highlight of the sleepover, and planning to bump into him the next morning over the breakfast table was something not taught in books. The entire night was spent in making the perfect plan without my girlfriend realizing what was going on in my pre-teen mind. The experience thrilled me beyond compare.

We travelled to a lot of the lesser known places and learnt so much. The tribal arts and crafts and survival stories of people in rough, remote terrain were like our daily dose of vitamins. We learnt to make the partridge pickle with the partridge my dad went hunting for. Once I stitched a beautiful white blouse for myself from a parachute that dad had got lying around in his room. It was the softest white fabric I had ever felt. He was quite unhappy when I told him I had cut up the parachute and there was enough fabric left over to stitch him a soft white night shirt too.

Every little thing added to my confusion. Eventually, I turned out to be much too wise for my years and grew up much too fast.

We always thought we were doing our best and carried on as we were until college. This was the first time I had to interact with civilians. These are people who did not belong to the services and they came from a different background from ours. These people's parents were businesspeople. They didn't do jobs; they owned the jobs and the companies.

They were third generation industrialists' kids. They drove cars, and the girls came to college in cotton candy-pink sneakers. They had so many clothes, shoes, bags, and hair clips. They travelled to Singapore, Europe, and the United States to shop. They lived in huge, sprawling mansions. They had a lot of money, something I had never seen in any large quantity.

Even as I managed the family accounts, funds disappeared as soon as they came in. Our lives looked great until it hit me that we had survived on very little cash compared to the real world.

Money was everything, not adventure; this was a new lesson. A feeling of deep inferiority washed over me overnight.

Even my classmates' grandmothers were different. These women drank brandy, smoked, and swam, while my illiterate grandmother could not even keep a count of her children. My classmates' grandmothers wore trousers and kept short hair, but my grandmother had a ratlike tail for hair. I had a theory that her nine children had pulled it out bit by bit; later it struck me that these rich grandmothers must have invested in wigs.

All the women, grandmothers, aunts, and teenage girls, visited salons for regular manicures and pedicures, while we were forced to scrub our feet with pumice stone and were convinced that this was the best thing for the skin.

Their dads wore Rolex. Mine owned a shockproof HMT watch from the army canteen, and when it stopped sometimes you had to tap it on the side of a table or bed for it to tick again. I would love to shock him with a Rolex today if he were alive.

The civilian kids had lots of cousins abroad, and they had either been or were about to go visiting them. They added 'darling' to everything. They were ultrarich businessmen's children, and they knew exactly what they were going to do. Their future jobs were waiting for them in one of their dads' many companies. I only knew I wanted to run away from my oppressive mom but didn't know where to go. Even after plotting many fantastic escapes, I realized I could not go far. I felt trapped on all sides.

More importantly, they all seemed to know who they were without any doubt. I was from a family of farmers turned officers, and my classmates were third generation businessmen who had acquired plenty of class and dough.

I realized showing off to them would mean nothing. My kind of adventure had no meaning in their lives. Their biggest adventure was to hit the club before 9 p.m. We had done it too, but this was different. They met to show off; we used to meet for pure entertainment.

My mom gave me her only sensible piece of advice when she found me crying and stitching a short skirt for myself from an old curtain. 'Why are we so poor?' I said. I felt really sorry for myself, as I was the only one in college who didn't have enough clothes to wear. She replied, 'Imagine how good you will feel when you have made it on your own, and they are just living off their dwindling inheritances and getting fat.' She had suddenly provided me with a double agenda: to be rich and to remain thin.

I could feel a sense of urgency of wanting to accomplish something really fast, while continuing to wear short skirts and watch the rich kids as they became fat and their wealth dwindled. I imagined myself living in their mansions, being served by their help and being driven around in their cars.

Just as I was getting ready to accept the challenge in earnest, I found myself in a serious relationship with a boy from college who came from an army background too. He shared my motivations, and both of us schemed to get rich somehow, remain thin, and stay sexy, a word he added to make it a threefold manifesto. 'Never become fat, just rich and sexy', was the motto. We dated for almost two years, until the day I kicked him and he had to walk home with his motorcycle.

With no one to plot and scheme with, the dreams were soon forgotten.

Not all dreams crashed like that one though. In fact, many of them grew wings in my footloose and fancy-free days after this break up. I started dating many of these rich, spoilt boys and experienced their lifestyle as an insider. I sorted some of them out. It was unintentional, but nevertheless I did them a favour. Despite having it all, they were not able to trap me; none had what it took to keep me with them for long periods. To see the good side of my personality, one had to be very patient, and nobody had it in him. The good was buried very deep. Often I didn't see it either.

I didn't have what it took to stay with anyone for long periods either, with no patience to wait endlessly for people to figure it out and catch up. I was always fast like the gazelle in everything I did.

I decided then to not compete with the other women as a girlfriend to these boys but to join the boys myself and move into their sphere. That was not easy either. Being a boy required serious money and at least a motorcycle. It was a man's world, I was beginning to realize. And for real acceptance, you had to be born male. We weren't kids anymore, but that didn't stop me from trying.

These boys loved to indulge in their favourite pastime, which was to drive really fast on their loud motorbikes. I had learnt to ride a bike with my boyfriend. What I owned, however, was a moped, and I rode it to college. Sometimes just for fun I would challenge one of the boys from college into a race. It was done for fun, not really to win, as the limited horsepower would not let me beat a motorcycle anyway.

But the guys and I loved this silly pretence, and once in a while some boy would let me beat him, especially if he liked me or was trying to get me to go out with him.

That stopped completely when one day I pushed the moped beyond its capacity to climb a hilly road. It started dismantling itself, part by part, in full view of some of the college gang. I had to chase all the nuts and bolts along the downhill road and collect them in a plastic bag that I used to hide under the seat for emergencies like this. Thankfully it could be repaired. I had managed to recover all the parts. After this incident I was definitely branded by as a girl who could not take care of her machine, and I could no longer pretend to be one of the boys.

I recall another instance of having to park the moped by the side of the road, as I just could not get it to start. It had stalled in the middle of the thoroughfare, and there was a huge bus just behind me honking away. I got off with as much dignity as I could, wheeled the moped to the side of the road, and then coolly got into the same bus that was now stopped by a red light. Eventually it delivered me to college.

I got my boyfriend of the threefold manifesto to take the moped to the mechanic, who said he just could not repair it any more. After that it was the boyfriend who used to drop me and bring me back from college, which was an upgrade of vehicle at least.

I compared my moped's unfortunate trip to the garage with my classmates' bikes getting regular service there in addition to jazzy new paint, side mirrors, seat covers, silencers, and other such stuff. It made me feel even worse.

I kept comparing and going nowhere. We had experienced luxury in the army life but it was only due to my dad, and now that he was living far away from us, we experienced the simple life in its true sense. The adventure was over. Life was dull.

Later we figured that having less money was a good thing, as it kept our feet firmly grounded in reality. Even though I dreamt big, there was no escaping the reality of paying those bills on that one meagre salary.

Slowly, the comparisons stopped and I just accepted that success wasn't going to happen as fast as I would like it to. The road was going to be long and hard, but I was confident I could do it eventually. The fire had been lit and the wood was dry. This was just in time for what was to follow soon.

Back then I was definitely a have not. The only time I did have it was when I sailed through college with top marks. Some of those who were so sure of themselves in year one were not really as powerful by the time we entered year three and they were far behind academically. I won through brains, if not through the green stuff.

This is when the equation shifted, and many of the rich folks who now lagged behind in their studies started coming to me for help just before their exams. I gave them tactics for studying smart in the short time they had. These three years saw me change from a nobody to a girl who was valued for her opinion, strong mind, ambitious attitude, and sense of humour; even though I did not originally belong to the rich club, I was now sought after and granted honorary membership.

The lack of wardrobe that I had felt in the first year evaporated. My innovations with the curtains and mom's saris actually had made me stand out among the girls who flashed FCUK T-shirts. How far can you go with an FCUK T-shirt, compared to a top with an exotic floral print? If you were to actually drape a printed floral curtain over yourself, the true beauty of the fabric would stand out. What we don't often appreciate as a piece of fabric hanging on a window, looks really nice on the body. I developed an admiration society for my wardrobe, and often people asked me where I got my clothes. I said I had a cousin who was an aspiring dress designer, and they went away impressed. I lied effortlessly at this point. I felt good to be in, and by now I had learnt all the rules to stay in. I invented many rich relatives who lived abroad, but it didn't matter to my peers now, as they liked me for who I was.

I felt good by the time I graduated, and many of them are my friends even today. I understood much later that they had never considered me inferior. They showed off because that is all they knew to do at that time. They didn't even realize that I was silently suffering in hell and feeling inferior. In fact they had liked me right from the beginning because of the spunk I exhibited. The wall had been raised from my side. As they approached me for studies and appreciated my wardrobe, I dropped this wall and realized what a long way I had come in these three short years.

We live in our own minds and we create our own reality. Life would have been much less of a struggle if only someone had guided me those days. Dad was away and it was much later I figured out that he had a drinking problem. That was the reason why mom and he had never agreed on anything. I saw my hero literally fall down in front of me. He just collapsed one day as we spoke. He was far gone. I was too anxious that something like this should happen in front of this lot that I was desperately trying to impress, so I never invited any of my friends home. I always stayed over at their houses. Even if I had to tutor them, I would go over. If it was late at night, I would get dropped outside our main gate and not let people come into the compound.

When parents lose their balance in any way, from alcoholism, a loss of money, or anything else, the children are lost. They can sense that something is seriously wrong. I read somewhere that parents leave their fingerprints on their children, who are like a clear glass when born. I carried these scars in the deepest part of me and somehow always managed to attract the guy that was addicted to his drink. We get bound by our patterns.

I now realized that my mom regretted not having had a choice of partner when she was married off to my dad. She always prompted my sister and I to speak our minds. We were being made into strong people, so we could answer back our parents and it was not considered bad behaviour as long as we spoke logically and not abusively. We were being trained to make our own mistakes and learn from them. My parents' not helping out as most other parents did was their conscious decision, though I always thought it was their indifference or lack of clarity.

They deliberately emphasized masculine qualities in my upbringing. My dad knew he was losing the battle with the bottle. My mom not objecting to this was her indirect acceptance that at any time she might become a young widow with two small girls to manage.

Soon he was no more. My father had a heart attack in his sleep at age fifty-one. Now I really was the man of the house. At twenty-one, I had just finished college and started my first job.

All other comparisons stopped then. The only thing or only one I could compare myself to was me. Nothing else mattered. That was actually the best thing I ever did. I made tremendous progress in that frame of mind.

My mom left the city and went back to the village in her ancestral home to manage on the pension that she was entitled to as a widow. I brought my sister to Bombay. She had to get a job immediately. I was fighting on behalf of all of us.

Obviously we had no savings to fall back on. I learnt then that money management is not just managing the expenses and the incomes for the month, but saving for the future as well. Saving had not been possible on the single income, and there was no inheritance. All our previous exposure came to our rescue, as first me and then my sister moved to Bombay with nothing more than a suitcase full of clothes and personal effects.

The two girls, who didn't count in the family of farmers are today talked about with great respect and often used as examples to inspire the younger generation. We haven't kept in touch with the cousins, but that is a different story. Some wounds are too deep to heal in a lifetime, even if inflicted unintentionally. Tender young souls sometimes find it too difficult to forgive those who may realize that the average child has an above average memory and that depth of feeling is inversely proportional to age. The older you are the more you are able to forgive, and even though today I feel different from what I felt twenty-five years ago, the child in me hated them for what they said or how they thought.

Once during the summer holidays, I heard my dad's brothers mock my mom and dad for not having a son. In my presence, they ridiculed my dad, saying that he would have to suffer paying dowry twice. My uncle said his own accounts would balance out, as he would get from his son's marriage as much or more dowry as he would give to his daughter.

My dad had looked very embarrassed. He hugged me close to his heart just that once and said, 'This one is my son.' Even as a thirteen-year-old I had wanted to slap or bite my uncle. I could not, so I carried it within.

In that instant I decided to never get married to a man who would want to receive money for marrying me. How could I be exchanged for money?

Somewhere the feeling of being inadequate deepened, and slowly I withdrew from my uncles, aunts, and cousins. Many such instances made me feel I was surrounded by a terribly prejudiced lot of people.

The person I wed should be glad I agree to marry him, I thought. I have stuck to my guns on that and just cannot understand why people believe that women are lesser human beings than men. I have seen so many men who just cannot survive without the woman in their lives, and often women thrive without any male support. The only reason for marriage should be love, nothing else.

Eighteen years have gone by since my dad died and my family had to move in different directions. My sister and I came to

Bombay and eventually Dubai, and mom went back to the farming family.

Soon after I was married. It lasted for almost a decade, but I still had that deep feeling of lack, even though all the basics were there.

I didn't really love the person I had married. We wed in haste, partly because he pushed me into it and partly because he never showed any interest in the dowry. He truly chased me for me. I liked that. I completely forgot my insight that one should not marry for any other reason but love. He said he loved me often enough, and in the rush of that short period, I never sat down to think if I loved him too.

My marriage is a good example of what happens when you wed for reasons other than love. We split up. He knew at some point that I didn't truly love him, and he sought love outside of the marriage. He still seeks it nine years after the divorce.

With the divorce, my old persona returned. I kept comparisons alive to keep the adrenalin pumped up at all times. I remembered the old manifesto: get rich; be thin and sexy. I had put on weight as a mom, and post-divorce I had not been able to eat anything. Automatically the weight started dropping. The 'be thin' part was easily achieved, and the other two would come when they would, I thought.

I kept focus on just my career and my child. I really connected with the spunk of my college days and the fire within. The desire to fight and not fall was strong. The flames burnt brightly now, and I started to feel the energy to achieve all that I set my mind on. I again excelled in every area. My single thought was to provide the best for my child. It kept me going, and I achieved everything beyond my wildest dreams.

The boundaries that we set for ourselves become our limitations. I decided to break all boundaries and see where life would take me. I made a clear vow that I would only compare myself today to myself of yesterday and improve on those areas that I perhaps got wrong before. I would appreciate myself for each and every little thing done well, because no one had ever done it for me. I started again, rather happy to have been set free.

My focus was on settling my family, this time my son and myself. My mom and sister stood by and supported me unconditionally, but my struggle was really my struggle, and they could not do anything to help clear the confusion that lay deep inside.

Material goodies flooded the house in no time. Clothes, jewellery, cosmetics, and shoes, household stuff and staff, were abundant. Happiness, good times and a certain sense of achievement all came into me. I began to realize my hidden strength which I had earlier suppressed as just a mother, a wife, and a daughter-in-law.

The sexiness came too. When you are sure of yourself and you know you are doing the right thing for the right reason, your aura develops a certain quality of calm confidence to it that the outer world sees as sexy. That is what happened to me. All that hard work and career focus got me job offers which doubled my salary, and I soon I was richer than I ever imagined I could be.

I achieved the threefold manifesto without even realizing it.

I have since then grown in all areas of life, and all previous feelings of lack have been replaced with abundance. Despite that, deep insights that money isn't everything keep zooming in.

Many of my friends are single parents and smart, well travelled women who have seen the worst and emerged as beautiful butterflies from all their trauma. They assure me that no one ever has it all. I am inclined to agree with them on most days, but there are moments when something deep within stirs and I feel that it has to add up to a full hundred percent, nothing less.

Maybe that elusive one percent which I feel is missing in my life is love. When I married I really did not have the time to find the right person, much less someone whom I thought I would love. Soon enough I let the fleeting thought go. I feel that real love finds you, and you don't have to chase it.

To my persistent question of 'Who am I?' I added the puzzle of 'What is love?' I realized that had been too busy being wise for the sake of our survival when most my age were busy being still so that love would find them.

Love just passed me by for the next twelve years. I had never been in love before. In the nine years of marriage, I did not love, and for three years after the divorce, I had no time for love. I placed my seven-year-old son in a boarding school to give him the same full life my parents had offered me. I missed him immensely and avoided getting back to an empty home after work. I started going out for the odd drink with friends.

I was simultaneously working on a plan to join my sister, who had moved to Dubai a few years ago to better her prospects both professionally and personally.

One night I was suddenly faced by real love staring with big eyes right into my face, and I didn't have the wisdom to recognize it for what it was. I felt confused and yet complete for the first time. It was inexplicable; I just could not put my finger on it. I felt like being a woman for just a bit and postponed the Dubai plan.

I started enjoying this man for who he really was, a child at all times focussing firmly on fun. The conversations grew and the juices flew. Then around six months later, I felt out of control and needed to get some equilibrium. I moved away to sort myself out.

Plan Dubai was put into action overnight, a knee-jerk reaction to avoid the strange stirrings. Later I identified this as the first time in my life that I ran away from something without having the courage to face it.

This was real love, the only thing I hadn't been taught to recognize or face. I had nothing to compare this feeling to, and in haste I put distance between us. I didn't realize what I was doing until it was much too late.

Isn't love like the butterfly that comes and sits on your shoulder just as you stop chasing it? Is it just a four-letter word? I had the rest of my life to find an answer to this, as my beloved married another.

Dubai added a new dimension to my comparisons. A friend and single parent who has been here for thirty years, educated me about the mascara that flows behind the veils. She tells me that I am better off without a man. She warns me that that is the wrong way to go even in my thoughts and reminds me of my days when I was with a man but not in touch with myself. She notes how much better a position I am in now.

Sometimes she manages to convince me. At other times, in the stillness and the darkness of the night, when I am truly alone, I reflect on what more could someone in my position want. Deep down there is a feeling of something really important that is still missing. I have overlooked something very critical in my search for money, success, looking good, and having it all.

Was it love? Was it the one I felt strange stirrings for and lost?

Ironically, this happening metropolis with all its glitz and glamour made the feeling of lack deeper every time I acquired something more. With each watch, rug, or new purchase I made, I felt I had become more hollow or shallow. The perfectly manicured trees and the beautiful malls spurred me to compare this life in Dubai to my earlier days in India, where the streets were lined with tiny kiosks and food carts created an obstacle course for drivers on the roads. Cats, pigs, cows, and hens frolicked in the garbage dump. I get nostalgic and miss those moments which were packed with action at all times. I did not appreciate it then.

I get my exercise now trawling the multitude of malls and come back heavier with all the food I ate out of sheer boredom, or lighter in the wallet because of an Omega watch I bought, also out of sheer boredom.

I see media personalities tying up and breaking up and wonder if romantic love is everything. I see people making big news about their relationships, and I wonder if that is really the be all and end all. Slowly I have been convinced that that elusive one percent will not be fulfilled by a man, at least for me, for now.

I know I miss that feeling of being loved.

I feel enough love for myself today and for all those that are around me, but I know I still crave it deeply from someone special. I had my chance in Bombay, and I walked away from it even before I could fully explore it.

Like the desire to gift my dad a Rolex, some wishes remain unfulfilled.

I used to compare myself to my best friend, who has been married for twenty-five years to her college sweetheart. I wondered why I didn't have that kind of relationship. Years of comparisons later, I finally got it. I did have everything that she and everyone else have. It's not as if she does not have her bad days with the man she loves. I felt things for my ex-husband in different proportions perhaps, but I had it all too. Even then something had been missing, I always knew that. He could not play the strings of my heart.

The difference is that my friend did not opt out. I did opt out. That was the lion in me.

When I look at my mom, who is now sixty-four, sleeping like a baby, I want to protect her and be there for her unconditionally, as opposed to eighteen years ago when I wanted to run away from her. A lot has changed for all of us since she was widowed at forty-six. I reflect on the life that she had to lead and suffer in silence so that her two daughters could bloom into the beautiful flowers of good human beings with strength, depth of character, and ability to come out winners in all situations. We were more precious to her than her life itself, but we never realized it.

I compare my mothering skills and wonder if I am doing a good job with my child. I peep into his room to find him slouched over the laptop. With headphones plugged in, he pounds words into the keyboard to express himself to his friends. Chat is his life. He is my life. He doesn't even realize it.

Then it comes to me. This life is not just mine. Although it was not my choice to be born, I have the choice to do with my life what I will. I feel a growing awareness of my need to get out and reach beyond these two people.

What will it take to make me really happy? This is the question I send out as I slip into bed. The universe eavesdrops into our thoughts, they say.

Of course I desire love from that someone special, I quickly add to the listening universe. And what else?

Our yesterdays have brought us here. Enough has been done for today. Let's see what tomorrow brings.

CHAPTER 3:

Seeking

Once the door of comparisons has been opened, it can only lead to seeking the things we figure out we are lacking. Sometimes it leads us to seek those things that make us feel fulfilled.

My earliest years saw me confused, though quite content with life. The main thing I felt lacking when I met the cousins was that their dads were always around while mine was not often nearby. I missed my dad. He was the only source of adventure in my life, and during those times that he was away I often sought activities to fill up my emptiness and somehow get the adrenalin rush that I was quite addicted to. Adventure made me feel fulfilled. It was the thing I went in search of all along.

Even in matters of love, I took the adventurous route just for the thrill of it. It started in college with the search for the perfect man.

—

First there was one. Then there were many. Sometimes it was a case of one too many men. Seeking at this time was great fun. Obviously the heart, the head, and the root chakra were operating independently of each other. What was not obvious even to me was that I was seeking to overcome my basic feeling of insecurity, which I encountered for the first time in my life in the college environment.

It started with one, the boyfriend of the threefold manifesto. This was a reasonably good relationship, and the connection was deep. The affection was easy to see, but it wasn't true love. He cared for me and was rather protective too. We broke up because he tried to control me. That was my only non-negotiable. Letting go of the control was not a concept in my version of the world.

After him there were many men. At one point in time I was seeing four guys at the same college. My belief that I needed a man emotionally vanished into thin air, and I was happy to explore my sexuality without any long term or serious expectations.

With each one I learnt a new lesson. My suspicion that men could not be trusted deepened, and I felt quite let down that my search didn't yield anything that made me feel better about myself.

Instead of the physical filling up, I started seeking by filling up my emptiness and inferiority with meaningless friendships and endless phone conversations.

That is when I went through my phase of attraction to very humorous guys, or merry men, as I called them. I met them through friends, and we got along very well over the days, spending many hours chatting over the old style of phone with a cord attached to the wall. Soon I found myself going out with these very funny men. A fantastic sense of humour was the only criterion to pass my test.

As with everything else I did, I was very thorough. I gave them a few quick and painless tests before I actually went out with them to ensure that they wouldn't lose their sense of humour when it was time to break up. They used to crack me up even as we ended our relationships. We can laugh about it even today.

My seeking reassurance through men, and perhaps for the first time doing something mindlessly, lasted for the three years of college and another year in Bombay when I first landed there. In Bombay I continued looking for answers with easy escapist behaviours like drinking, bingeing, and smoking hash.

I got my professional life right all of the time, no matter what else was going on in other areas of my life.

After a lot of playing doctor, one day I actually landed up at a clinic. The cheaper abortion clinic I visited the month prior had not done a thorough job, and I had to have the procedure repeated. That made me stop and use my head for a bit.

My husband to be entered the picture just then. I was feeling let down by my search, and he came ready with the ring and words of love from the depths of his soul, which no one else ever told me in the same manner. He never uttered the magic word dowry, and that only eased the seduction. I agreed to marry him.

I truly stumbled after my divorce, having made some foolish decisions earlier. I was a little afraid of getting up and starting to run again, lest I fall flat on my face and never recover. I sought quick and easy comfort.

A lot of people look to their parents for support even when they are forty-five years old. I was thirty then, and I did the same. Mom and I had always been at odds with one other, and she watched me helplessly. She took over day-to-day responsibilities for me and my son and reminded me to pray. My sister in Dubai tried to talk me out of the bad phase, but all she ended up with was huge phone bills. No one could reach me in the lonely cell I had imprisoned myself in.

I had to focus on my son's emotional needs and had really no time to attend to myself. I started my emotional deep freeze around that time.

Children are usually dependent on their peer groups, but my son was not even five years old, too young to understand what had happened and why his dad was suddenly not around. The neighbours' gossip added to my problems. More than once the bully personality from my childhood days came out to settle things. 'Shut up' was my favourite phrase. I muttered it under my breath when folks looked at me with pity.

I made the sad realization that this is a very male dominated world. I also saw that women enable this system by giving away their power. I made up my mind never succumb to that mindset.

My desire for quick solutions to my problems has often prompted me to seek help from all kinds of people who brand themselves experts.

The expectation of winning has often been a stumbling block for me. As a child, I was always an ace student, but around age twelve my interest in academics wavered for just a bit as I started noticing boys in a different light.

One afternoon after an exam I was walking back from school and feeling a little disillusioned at having submitted a bad paper. Near my house I noticed a crowd on the street. Kids and servants surrounded a holy man and an overly decorated cow. I paused to see what was going on. I learnt from the kids that the cow could predict the future. I thought this might be a good way to determine the result of my exam, so I asked the holy man if the cow knew the answer I sought. The crowd got excited when they heard my question. All eyes were on the holy man, who nodded and said that the cow could easily predict my exam results.

Very impressed and really curious to know if I had passed, I asked the cow for the answer. Then the holy man revealed that the cow only spoke when she was offered money. I dug into my school bag and tried to find the one rupee that had been given to me that morning as tuck shop money. Then remembered I had spent it. By then the holy man was losing patience, and I asked him to wait just a minute for me to rush home and come back with the fee. The cow did not answer for anything less than five rupees, the man informed me. I worried about raising this huge sum of money, but I was nevertheless determined to have my answer. I ran home before my opportunity to know my exam results slipped away.

My mom was in the habit of leaving the main door open when it was time for me to return from school, and I found the door ajar. I knew by then where the money would come from. I slipped in like a thief and headed straight to the altar where all the Hindu gods were displayed and some small amount of money was kept as a daily offering. It was believed that if you offered money to the gods they would multiply it for you.

I counted five rupees from the many coins there and rushed back to the crowd. I handed the money to the holy man and waited for the cow to answer my question. The crowd had grown in size during my quick exit. The man told me to stand facing the cow and whisper the question in the cow's right ear. The holy man took his place behind me and chanted some mantras[3] while raising a saffron cloth with both his hands very quickly. At exactly the same moment, as if it understood all the mantras, the cow raised its head to the skies and then looked at its own feet. The cow had said yes, the holy man proclaimed.

I was elated at the knowledge that I would pass the exam. The crowd cheered, and I felt victorious already. Everybody touched the holy cow on its forehead for blessings and luck.

---

3 *A sacred verbal formula repeated in prayer, meditation or incantation, such as an invocation of a god, a magic spell or a syllable or portion of scripture containing mystical potentialities.*

This was my first tryst with prophecy. No one knew what I had done that afternoon.

When I got home and mom asked me how the exam had been, all earlier feelings of doubt vanished. I confidently said that I was certain that I would pass with decent marks. When the results were announced, I learned that I did pass the exam. It reinforced my faith in the cow and inclined me to believe in a lot of other weird stuff later on.

This particular incident left a very deep mark on me, which I addressed with my mom recently. The immense pressure that I felt in childhood and the very high benchmark which I was never allowed to lower made me push myself to the edge every time, and not always in a positive manner. It also made me look for reassurance from external sources, as I had received none within the home.

I explained to mom that if I had thought she and dad would not be terribly disappointed if I had occasionally done badly in school or other activities, I would most certainly not have sought such measures as holy men and their fantastic cows. My mom still cannot see what my point is and says there was no way she could have my sister and I do poorly in school or any other activity. She explained that the pressure of not having a son made it even more important that we be brought up successfully to prove that girls are as good as boys, if not better.

I am shocked at her logic, and at the same time I try to empathize with her situation as it might have been in those days. Why didn't they just have another child and try their luck at a son? The Indian government promoted family planning in that era and each family stopped at two kids. Our poor country had a big population and someone had to do something to control it, including my obedient parents at great cost to me.

All arguments stop when we reach this kind of insightful point in the conversation, and we settle for a cup of tea in silence.

Too much water has passed under the bridge. This lesson is well learnt, and I am mindful that my son never feels any kind of obligation to do well all the time. Coincidentally, he happens to be an excellent student. When he does come home with a bad grade, we actually tell him to enjoy this low moment so that he can experience it for what it is.

Like everything else, this too shall pass. What does this moment matter when placed in a five-year perspective?, my best friend often says. She is right. It shouldn't always be about excelling; it should be about enjoying. I learnt that rather late in life.

The desire to overcome today's pain and to move ahead made me seek out those who I thought had the answers, as I did in childhood.

The holy men returned in full force from far and near. They followed me everywhere, and I loved them. They gave me hope, the best kind of reassurance. Tomorrow was going to be better.

Tomorrow will come any day now, I said to myself. It went on like that for many years.

I thought I would cheat and get a sneak peek into my future. I started searching for the answers through holy men. The fear of rushing in was quite strong now, and a calculation always made me feel I was on firm territory. I went deeper and deeper into predictions. I started reading the newspaper with the last page first, as they do in Arabic. The horoscope was the first column that I turned to.

At thirty-three, I saw real love walk into my life. I met him for the first time at a restaurant in Bombay called Under the Over. He had the biggest eyes I have ever seen, so clear and clean and unpretentious that I could look right down into the depths of his soul. His voice was so soft I could hardly hear what he said. And there was music to it.

The butterfly had landed, and I was not prepared. I felt dizzy and overpowered. In no time at all he got under my skin and I knew that this would never be over for me.

He made me feel out of control in a strange way that I had never felt before. I wanted to be just a woman with him, nothing else. I was in love, a feeling I didn't begin to understand until much later.

Instead of just being still and enjoying it for what it was I felt inadequate and unable to handle my feelings. I tried to push it away from me, saying I didn't need it. I moved to Dubai.

I searched for a new beginning, not realizing that everything I was looking for was coming to me on its own. All I needed to do was stop searching and just let it happen. I could not let it be. I needed to be in control back then. Instead of waiting patiently for things to happen naturally and allowing them to grow, I chose to move away. I believed the distance would resolve the issue. It did, for him; he got married to another within a year of my move. I had a sense of the earth shifting beneath my feet as I heard the news from him. I realized I was hopelessly in love, even as I tried to absorb what he said amidst the haze and spinning in my head.

I repented at leisure for the next three years that it took me to get over him. I added on layer upon layer of unresolved drama to my life, when all along I really truly desired was to clear the mess and float effortlessly in the river of life.

I had everything that I didn't care about and had lost the only thing that mattered to me besides my son, I realized with each passing day.

Despite having everything in Dubai, I was not happy. I still didn't know who I was, and I was willing to travel far and wide to get that answer now. I knew that I was missing love, but it had to be a special kind of love, something more than love, I thought.

I discovered then that money isn't everything and that money cannot define you or bring you to your true love.

When a few of the predictions that the astrologers made came true, my belief was reinforced. I was now spending substantial sums of money to support this interest. One thing led to another. It started with the horoscope column and then progressed to an astrologer who read the past and future of my entire personal horoscope. I didn't care about the present. That was what I was running away from.

I sought help from these holy men before taking any action. They not only gave me a propitious date and time for any assignment, but they advised the colour of clothes I should wear too and what direction I should face to ensure a successful outcome. They gave me rituals to complete before taking on a new project. Not desirous of leaving anything to chance, I took it all upon myself to tackle any surprises life should try to throw my way.

I learnt some Sanskrit slokas[4] and started chanting them as suggested by the holy men. These are the everyday Hindu prayers that were common knowledge to my cousins growing up. I had never received a religious education, but I accepted the prayers now.

After a while, surely and surely things started improving. My belief in these men deepened, and I wouldn't take a single step on my own. Formerly a strong minded woman, I became a clinging person. They had unbelievable power over me, they read the insecurity in my eyes.

I kept looking for answers from outside. These people pursued me even when I deliberately stayed away from them. They smelled my fear.

It was as if the cosmos threw them in my direction. Even on flights, the person sitting next to me would pull out a piece

---

4 *verse of two lines in praise of God.*

of paper and start drawing a horoscope chart with its familiar rectangle enclosing a diamond and a cross within. The addict in me would peer at the sheet of paper and start a conversation with the unsuspecting passenger. Before the end of the flight, he might have given a free consultation in reply to my many questions. If he was an astute businessman, he might give me his phone numbers and say that the severe problem in my chart could only be resolved through a ritual which, I would learn later, turned out to be really expensive.

Nothing deterred me. I was determined to clean out all the wrong planetary placements in my birth chart with the help of these men. The planets were really slow to respond, but for the first time I performed religious rites and rituals like my cousins did. My objective was not even close to their goals of achieving spirituality or something that fantastic. I performed them mindlessly in hope that the planets would be appeased and perhaps jump from one house in my chart and move to another and take all my problems with them.

If all the astrologers and other experts that I followed for nine years simply returned their fees, I would be able to do something worthwhile for some really needy people. What's gone is gone, but at least the lessons remain.

From thereon I explored in depth everything from aura reading to stone therapy, gemology to angel whispering, tarot to crystal ball gazing, palm readers, face readers, thumb print readers, and acupuncture. I even heard about mole readers and diviners of tea leaves, but I haven't managed to meet any as yet.

Each study added to my awareness about life. I realized how nothing is complete in itself, and each is just a tiny part of the whole. It took a long time to figure this out, painfully sampling each one and waiting for the result to materialize, or sometimes not.

I learned that there are no absolutes. Nothing is complete in itself. Everything is a part of something. Everything is linked to something else. Nothing is independent. This is like a giant spider web that will completely suck me in, I thought.

When I turned to gemology and precious stones, I was recommended to wear rings of different colours and stones by each new holy man I encountered. I finally ended up with rings of ruby, pearl, blue sapphire, emerald, diamond, yellow sapphire, pink sapphire, and amethyst. My colleagues used to mock me and ask if I wished for more fingers so that I could wear a couple more rings. I wore eight rings at that time, one on each finger. The directives of all my holy men, and one holy woman, contradicted each other, and finally I gave up trying to understand. I just put on all the rings at one time.

Overnight my bank balance fell and my bling quotient soared under the hot desert sun. I am sure I could have been spotted from even Mars as an extremely shiny object on planet Earth with the naked Martian eye.

About two years later I met a rudraksh[5] merchant. He told me to just remove all the rings and wear the blue sapphire and the emerald. I have felt better ever since. My son teases me and asks me to remove these two precious rings as well. He wants me to cope with the normal risks of life for just a day to see what really goes wrong. I can't take a chance, I tell him.

I met my guardian angels through a channel who spoke to them and received their messages. They told me to just relax and let things be. The angels are really here with us all the time. We don't see them, but they help us whenever we seek their assistance, she told me. We all have our own personal

---

5 *Rudraksh beads are the material from which garlands of 108 beads are usually made. It is a bead as well as a rosary, used for repetitive prayers. Asian Yogis and Monks found that merely wearing the rudraksh beads gave them astonishingly tremendous amount of tranquility, concentration which helped them meditate for a long period of time with spectacular control over their mind.*

guardian angels, and it is possible for us to connect with them, but it took me a long search to find them. I now connect with them through meditation regularly. I have them by my side always, and I am a new me now.

I moved into exploring the energies that surround us. I looked into feng shui, numerology, graphology, and vastu. I changed my name twice and my signature too. The only thing I would not change was my attitude. I was not willing to let go of the past and I kept mulling over it. I was trying to control a future that was not yet there. I was avoiding the perfect present.

I studied hypnotherapy and learnt to take people to their past lives. I went to nine of mine as well. I armed myself with techniques like EFT – Emotional Freedom Technique, NLP – Neuro Linguistic Programming, Time Line Therapy (R), and crystal healing.

I gained short-term clarity and a feeling that all will be well, but my confusion deepened each time I widened my search with another one of these studies.

I met so many practitioners, and they all had the same message for me in almost exactly the same words: You have nothing to worry about. You are God's child. You are going to do something fantastic.

This made it worse. I had one more question now. I intensified my search for that person who could tell me exactly what this fantastic thing would be. No one had the answer. They all just asked me to perform some more complicated rituals.

One of them told me to feed a cow and a dog every day. In India that is fine. I encountered lots of cows, dogs, pigs, and hens just as soon as I stepped out of my house. In Dubai it was a real challenge. I was nearly in tears when I told my sister how upset I was that they don't allow cows to roam the streets of Dubai. She cried too, from hysterical laughter. What makes me do all this, she often laughs at me. I don't know. I just believe.

I asked my friend why I looked for that one elusive thing when I already had pretty much everything I could want. It's about going to the next level, she told me wisely. That is what we all aspire for. What about the person who has everything then? I countered. Does anyone ever have everything? she asked. Who has everything? Those who have money and love realize that it is not enough. My friend and I are both single parents, and we think romance is our missing ingredient, but those who have romance miss something else. I know what she is trying to communicate. Everyone has to go on their own search for their missing piece.

In my searching, there was a time when I worshipped the rising sun by facing the East and pouring out water first thing in the morning and chanting some auspicious Sanskrit words. It must have satisfied the sun gods, because within a few days of having done that I was miraculously saved from a severe calamity. In fact I had a windfall. I managed to sell my property in Bombay at peak rates, just days before the crash of October 2008.

Someone told me to pray all day for forty days and eat vegetarian every Tuesday and Saturday during that period. I obliged. My mom was thrilled when she heard this. I was advised to keep a prayer on my lips as often as possible in that period, I tried my best to comply. I would wake up in the night with a start and feel as if I had cheated by sleeping instead of praying. The fast was easy really. I was allowed to eat only certain fruits and milk on the fast days. This actually led to clear skin and a glowing complexion. I called it a detox of the body.

The gods were waiting to show me the way, but first I had to pray, I had been told. I prayed from 5 a.m. to about 7 a.m., and then in the shower and during my drive to work. I chanted the mantras again in the car while driving to meetings. The radio in my car hadn't been turned on for a long time now, except for the occasional bhajan or holy songs. If my sister, mom, or son spoke to me, I would nod or shake my head in response, as my lips were silently praying all the time.

Closer to my fortieth birthday, I noticed a sense of peace descend upon me. Nothing bothered me. I knew now I had God on my side, or at least I knew that I was on God's side, and that was like agreeing to be part of the winning team.

I mellowed. I softened as a person. Many people would just walk up to me to have a conversation with no agenda. A sense of having opened the door to the meaning of life came upon me. I called it detox of the mind.

I stopped the excessive prayers and continued seeking, this time through reading. The bhajans[6] and holy songs opened the door to meditative tapes. I wanted theory now. Through reading I came to understand that this too shall pass. I was indirectly reassured that others have been here too. I started gravitating towards people who seemed to have found that elusive missing piece, and I tried to absorb their messages. I felt inspired to follow, but it was really difficult to do what they suggested.

I ended up feeling more and more confused. They made it all sound so simple in the books. When I sat down to do what they said, I could not even close my eyes and shut out the sounds for a few seconds. They spoke of the silent mind and meditation as if it was an afternoon siesta after having drunk a lot of wine on a rather warm day. In my eagerness to retain the feeling of calm that the forty days of prayerful living had brought me, I had aimed too high. I needed to step back, start over, and perhaps go slower this time. Patience had to be nurtured. It was the mother of all virtues.

After a long and wasted effort to search for my identity, true love, and prophecy, I truly gave up. I got a sense of looking in all the wrong places. Perhaps I might have the answers to what I will be looking for in my next life, I tried to reassure myself. Past life had taught me that the soul lives on even though the body dies.

---

6 *Hindu devotional songs.*

Past life regression showed me a lot of bad deeds that I had accumulated in previous lives. There is a higher keeper of accounts who makes you pay for all your sins, not as punishment, but more like lessons to be learnt before moving ahead, my guru said.

I thought my past life sins were probably blocking my present life and preventing me from finding the missing piece in the jigsaw puzzle of my life. I decided to clear the negative karma of the nine past lives that I had seen in my regression therapy sessions. I made a plan to visit my birthplace in Dehradun, and start again from there.

I took seriously a holy man's suggestion that taking a dip in the Ganges to wash off all my sins would be a good place to start. It fitted in with my original plan of a new beginning, I rationalized to my exasperated sister and now even my son, who could not understand my need for me to seek through such means instead of trusting my natural instincts. I had everything now, he rationalized from his thirteen-year-old perspective, the best of all possible worlds. I had just him to love and take care of, and when he was older he would take care of me, he said. What was the need to start all over again? He could not quite grasp it from my perspective.

The trip to Dehradun was just so beautiful. I visited the house that I had been born in and thought back to the time when I started my journey on this planet. It seemed so far away and such a long journey only to come back to the same spot almost thirty-nine years later.

I gained tremendous insights just standing at the spot where I played as a carefree child. Was I ever a carefree child, I tried to recall? I could not get a picture at all. I called my mom, who had not travelled with us, from outside the house to ask her to describe it. She narrated things that made me cry, like the little road where she walked me in my pram in the evenings. The road was still there. This place had not been touched by progress.

Feeling refreshed, I was quite motivated to forget the past and do everything right from now on. My sister and son, who had accompanied me, both saw a shift in my persona at that moment.

The next day we drove to Rishikesh, a place nearby at the foothills of the Himalayas, to take a holy dip in the Ganges. The water was flowing so fast that the current could carry people off quite easily. It was freezing. I entered the river and prayed for all my sins to be washed away. Dip, dip, dip. I went in and out three times. I felt cleansed. It is difficult to describe the feeling, but the feeling of having washed off my sins was quite immediate. I felt lighter as I came out. The weight had lifted.

As we got out of the water and walked back towards the car to make the journey back to Dehradun and finally back to Dubai, a tiny shop attracted me. Just then the door of the shop opened and a holy man stepped out. My sister shook her head, signalling a strong no. I had decided when I started afresh to trust in myself, but this was too much of a temptation to a recovering addict: a holy man in a holy place. He appeared to have a direct link with god. I was unable to get into the car. I ignored my sister and my son and stepped into the shop. Quite by accident, I found the rudraksh. The shopkeeper had the gentlest voice and had soon managed to get my sister and son interested in the rudraksh as well. An hour later, I walked out of the shop with my magical bead around my neck.

It is believed in Hindu mythology that the tears of Lord Shiva touched the earth when he opened his third eye and sprouted into the rudraksh tree. Rudraksh beads, which are seeds from these trees, have almost magical powers. No sooner had the bead touched me than I felt a sense of completeness. This is also when my life, which was already good, absolutely became the best that it could ever be. I saw that only in hindsight a few months later.

I have tried routes and suggestions from so many people, but no one had ever suggested this magic bead to me. It is the single most powerful thing that has ever touched my skin. The moment I wore it I felt a sense of completeness that I had never before felt in my life. I was one. I am not saying I got enlightened, just that I could simply be myself.

Rudraksh to me is what a diamond is to most other women. It calmed my restless mind and gave me a sense of wanting to be still. I knew that my search had been successful. I had opened a door to myself. I felt confident that I would no longer seek external sources. I would have faith in myself from that point on. I finally understood that I had been looking in all the wrong places. By putting aside the desire to have all the answers immediately, I started living in the today.

Realizations came slowly. The search is about keeping control or letting go. When we stop searching, we let go of the control we like to have. It's about looking internally versus externally. We are complete from the inside, but we look to the outside for completion. We need a really powerful torch to look inside ourselves and a powerful vacuum cleaner to suck out all the muck that we find within. They haven't made that yet, so we have to clean our insides bit by bit, ever so gently. To make sure that we do not collect more negativity, we have to build an invisible shield around our auras.

Mindless searching can sometimes lead us to the right spot, as happened to me with the rudraksh. It could have been a shorter search if I had received formal Hindu education and learnt the regular lessons my cousins learnt. They had been aware of the rudraksh for many years, but I ended up going from one source to another aimlessly, whereas I should have received a formal religious training. Faith keeps us grounded and prevents the drifting that I experienced. Faith first in an external object translates over a period of time into faith in ourselves, even as the world around us crashes. The external object does not have to be a god. It could be our parents, our peer groups, or whoever we lean on for support. They help us to find ourselves when we are feeling lost.

In the end, we have to accept that the answers lie within. How rooted are we? The rudraksh is not a magical bead that can lift every cloud for us, but in touching our skin it somehow changes our vibration and gives us peace. Often we seek because we are not at peace.

If you know your identity, the search for the missing piece is easier, faster, and I guess less painful. If you don't know yourself, as was my case, then the search is longer and directionless, like a ship without its sails being tossed about in a storm. You don't know what to anchor into.

Think of the number of times you have really achieved things with a peaceful state of mind, as opposed to the times you stressed yourself out. When did you get a better result? I know the answer for myself and have discovered the state of mind that works for me. I get more done in less time, and I don't waste time in useless activities and worry about the future or the past. It is in the living now, peacefully, that we achieve a better tomorrow.

What I found through the rudraksh, others may find through meditation or some other anchor. Ultimately it is important to be at peace to find the thing that you seek. The calm state of mind brings you to your purpose faster.

CHAPTER 4:

Clinging

Attention from the opposite sex came easy. Sometimes I ended up in a relationship as part of my adventure seeking. Never did any of my boyfriends move me from the inside, even my husband, until I happened to bump into the one person who turned my world upside down. He gave me the gift of feeling love from the depths of my soul for the very first, and perhaps the only time in this life. I clung on for dear life.

This part of my life taught me the one word I never thought I would make a part of my vocabulary: regret. After doing all the wrong things to the right person and realizing it much too late, regret stayed with me like an unwanted guest.

The marriage gone wrong definitely bothered me. I felt strangely cheated, not just because he had slept with another, but largely because I gave up my prime time from twenty to thirty years of age for this man. He had fallen on his knees and resorted to all kinds of things to get me to marry him, I did believe when I entered into it that it was for keeps.

The failed marriage also created a lot of external stress. Just around that time, I found the story of the Bobbits very inspiring. I didn't like the idea of being dumped by my ex-husband, but that act hurt the ego, not the heart. I didn't feel love with him, though I did sometimes wonder about it in the three years following the divorce. I was not really sure what love was then.

Then one day I was absolutely certain that that what I felt for my ex-husband was not love at all. This was the real thing.

We have seven chakras[7] in our bodies. The heart charka is the fourth, and there are three above it and three below. The heart chakra lies exactly in the centre.

That is where love hit me: right in the middle, the heart of the matter. That is when it hit me too, in what I considered to be midlife. I was thirty-three years old.

Theory has it that the heart chakra opens fully around the age of twenty within most of us. That is perhaps what a lot of people believed in the days around the time my mom was married. In that era most couples wed in their early twenties. That was considered as a good age for a union to take place, as the acceptance of another into our heart is very easy then. Those were the days of arranged marriages.

7   translates as wheel, disc or turning. The Chakras are said to be "force centers" or whorls of energy permeating, from a point on the physical body, the layers of the subtle bodies in an ever-increasing fan-shaped formation (the fans make the shape of a love heart). Seven major chakras or energy centers (also understood as wheels of light) are generally believed to exist, located within the subtle body.

My heart chakra seemed to have opened rather late. I confused it with a midlife crisis, not knowing any better. It was about sharing and true love, but I didn't understand either of those emotions. I thought it was a crisis to be resolved. That was well in line with my abilities.

Instead of going with the flow, I fought it. By the time I figured out that it was love I felt, I desperately clung to him, the true love. It was too late by then. Unknowingly, I had pushed him to the point of no return. Before him, I had never experienced these emotions or such intensity in my life.

I truly should have just let it be. It was a lesson that I had to figure out completely on my own in the three years after we broke up. Love has to grow. I was force feeding someone who was not hungry. Ironically, that was the best time of my life.

Our first meeting was the only dinner we ever dined out. Before this first meeting, I had spoken frequently on the phone with him for about six months. I was strangely attracted to his musical, laughing, and youthful voice from the first time I called him.

He was one of the funniest people that I ever spoke with. He quickly brought my completely forgotten sense of humour back to life. Without even realizing it, I was flying like a bird. My colleagues and friends were really happy to see me come out of my lonely prison cell. They complimented me on this progress, but no one knew what to attribute it to, not even me.

I was just so happy to be speaking with him. I found a sense of calm from him, something that I figured I had been looking for. I didn't know how to do it for myself, so I would call him. We spoke about everything initially. It was such a safe and wonderful feeling having him on the other side of the phone. The word 'caution' did not enter my thoughts at all.

When we first met, he had no idea what a lost soul I was. At that time I had consciously decided to keep away from my earlier lot of friends. They had started giving me looks of pity and unsolicited advice, even though I wasn't looking for their help or sympathy. They needed gossip, and I refused to provide them with anything. I was closing the old and moving into the new.

I formulated a new plan to take me on the correct path into the future. I wanted no more hurdles, just a smooth and easy ride from now on. I had achieved my earlier threefold manifesto to a large extent, and I needed something more mature to replace that in order to make it in this world.

Alone, and in a rather wise state of mind this time, I made a very intelligent fourfold pathway for myself. I got real with myself and acknowledged that I was at the crossroads of life. The number four appealed to me. It was the number of directions on a compass. It would always remind me of the time when I had been at the crossroads, looking for direction, I thought. I prioritized my goals in the order that they would need to be addressed.

1. Forget the past.

2. Make new friends.

3. Start a new life.

4. Never get married again.

These four sentences haunt me even today. None of them worked out quite the way I imagined they would. I broke each of them in exchange for a lot of pain.

I first knew my lover as the person who could get any book that I was looking for. I was trying to find Jeffrey Archer's *A Prison Diary*, and I just didn't know which store would have it. It had been reviewed in the newspapers the same morning. I called him on the number my colleague gave me, and he sent the book to my office the very next day. This is a really convenient way to get books, I thought. I usually knew what book I was looking for, and a trip to the bookstore was not top of my to do list. I saved his number for future reference.

Soon we started talking on the phone, first for books that I wanted for my son who was at boarding school, then for titles for me. These brief requests for books soon graduated into small talk with a lot of 'How are you?' and 'What's new?' We had never met.

I had blocked out most of my pals as a way to not be reminded of the past, and he happened to be a new friend. I started this acquaintanceship as a new me, with no past baggage. That was the first point on the plan anyway. I ended up crying to him more than I have to anybody else in this entire world.

Looking back, he made no references to my past at all. Before I knew it, I was telling him my entire life story over the phone. The first time I narrated how I had made a shambles of my life, I went on for an hour or more. Only when I paused for a breath did I look at the clock to see that it had been over an hour. I was shocked. I hadn't spoken for that long in years.

After that I never looked at the clock when I dialled his number. I enjoyed him and that was all I cared to know. I was beginning to break my very deliberate fourfold pathway already.

I could go on for as long as he could hold on to the phone. He was the only one who could listen to me for an hour without uttering a word. After the hello, or sometimes even before it was said, I launched into the narrative. He was polite enough to listen and never interrupt. Only when I had truly finished would he say that someone had been waiting outside his office for the last forty-five minutes and would it be alright to talk later.

He was doing for me what perhaps a counsellor would have done. I doubt if even they would have displayed this kind of patience. On hanging up I felt complete release at having poured out all the exciting and sad highlights of my life as well as the mundane contents of my afternoon.

I always thought that I would keep the past out of our next conversation. I wanted talk about normal events, as we had at first, but I couldn't seem to help myself. I had never encountered such a patient person before. I had not finished all my past stories even in the next six months.

He got to know more about me than those I had spent the most time with, including my sister, who had been my confidante, especially after the divorce. Now she called me once a week instead of every day, but she was happy that I sounded happy. I told her about this guy, whom I had never met, and how we were just friends on the phone. That comforted her and me too, strangely enough.

No sooner had I said those words to my sister, than I realized they were not true. We were not just friends. At least, I wasn't. I had become very attached to this man on the phone and hadn't even met him once. I only knew his mobile number and nothing else, not even his family name. It was weird. I felt a connection as if I had known him before.

I just could not understand how he had managed to get me to do everything that I had stopped doing: to open up again, to smile again, to not give a damn again, to be happy again, to trust a man again, to trust myself again, to laugh from the bottom of my heart again. I learnt gentleness, perhaps for the first time. He inspired all this without ever contributing many words of his own.

This strange pull I felt for him was indefinable. I stayed awake entire nights and attempted a serious step-by-step analysis of this thing we had on the phone. I couldn't make sense of it.

I finally put it down to midlife crisis. People in my position sometimes jumped on the very first thing that crossed their path, I convinced myself, but somewhere this did not ring true. I never felt like meeting any of the men who had asked me out before.

That first time I called him with a request for a book and I heard his 'hello' on the phone, I felt something move inside. I have been a phone person all my life, for both friendships and work. No voice ever got me craving for more as his tinkling, jovial voice did.

Ironically, he spoke very little. In trying to hear more and more of him, I chatted him up for an hour at a time, several times each day. We conversed while I drove to work, when I drove for meetings, and as soon as I drove back to my lonely home. We spoke after his dinner or sometimes as late as 2 a.m. after he returned from an evening out. Actually, I spoke. He listened. I kept calling back on various pretexts to hear his voice, and slowly he spoke too.

The best times were when he would read passages from books to me late at night. I asked him to read more and more until he said there was no more left to read. The book has no more pages he would say. I had not read for a long time and enjoyed the process of being educated by him. When he spoke he had the right words. Words had always appealed to me, and he combined them so well with his sense of humour.

His parents went visiting family overseas, and he was alone for a month or more. I thought he would ask me out. At that point I hadn't felt curious enough to ask him for a picture or email one of mine.

This was a really simple case of two people getting along. What was there to not get along about, actually? He never said anything confrontational. He was always polite and a good listener. There were times I tested him to check if he just put the phone on loudspeaker and chimed in once in a while to show his attendance. The moment I stopped speaking and said, 'So?' he immediately replied with a thoughtful answer. He had to be listening.

He often made fun of me. 'How could anyone talk so much?' he asked. 'How can anyone listen to so much?' I countered, and we laughed. He made being silly so easy. As the comfort grew, the fun and games came in.

The first few times he played with me I was not sure if he was serious. I had hardly heard him speak, and when he did it was all fun. Nothing serious ever crossed his lips. Sometimes I asked him, 'Don't you have any issues?' He would say, 'No', he didn't, 'it takes up too much energy'. Did he never feel angry towards anyone? Apparently not. It was too good to be true. Wake up right now, I tried to warn myself. He was the perfect man, but they hadn't been invented yet, I knew from experience.

His ability to lift my serious conversations to a light-hearted level was what kept me hooked. At the same time he never took what I said lightly. He waited for me to pour out all my angst, then magically, with a short phrase, he transformed the mood of the entire previous hour of conversation. Just at the thought of him finding the humour in the drama of my life, I broke out into uncontrollable laughter. Before I knew it, I fell in love. It was seduction of the mind. We hadn't met in person yet, and I don't think he even realized what was happening at my end.

Later, I asked him why he didn't reject me after all the stuff I had shared with him, He said it was because all my stories of the past ended up having a moral. More importantly, I saw even the most negative moments as lessons to be learnt and not as punishments. This appealed to him. The chemistry we shared was huge, there was no doubt about that. No one can tolerate anyone for such long periods if the basics don't gel.

I talked to him like I would to a family member. I mentioned things like how much I cried when I left my son at boarding school. It started with the defining moments of my life and soon went into details. I wondered why I spoke with him. He didn't add anything to my thinking or change my perspective. He just listened. Couldn't I have done that with myself in a mirror?

Sometimes all I could hear when we were on the phone were the background sounds of his environment. The street sounds of Bombay were familiar to me, and sometimes I heard his dad chat with him just before bed. Sometimes I overhead his neighbours' parrot outside his office, sometimes I listened to his car. Wherever he went, I did too.

Up until our very last day together, his voice had the ability to send tiny tremors all over my body. His voice is soft, and I am quite hard of hearing myself, so I had to strain to catch every word. I thought that that was his way of ensuring I paused in the conversation to actually listen to what he said. Ten minutes once every few days had become four to five hours daily in less than six months. I had so much to say, and he had such a listening ear.

We never tried to meet at all during the first six months. After we finally met, we barely left one another's side.

I had been asked out in the past three years and had absolutely refused to even go out for a coffee with anyone. Then I found him. The best part was that he never showed any interest in asking me out. It was nice to know a guy who didn't want anything from me and didn't chase me.

Around the six-month mark, I started to wonder why he never asked me out. Perhaps he was waiting patiently for all the emotional clutter of my past to pour out before we started being more than friends, I thought.

I used to think of him as a doctor's prescription of 3TDS, which means 'to be taken orally three times daily after meals'.

Sometimes the doses were really close together and without any meals in between. I guess I generated my energy to survive with tongue movement, just like a windmill makes electricity.

I felt better just speaking with him. The thought of not being asked out went away just as soon as I heard his voice. He was always a phone call away, so why did I need to be taken out for a coffee? I thought to myself.

That didn't stop me from wondering if something was really wrong with him. Maybe he was a hunch-back. Immediately, I brushed that thought aside. Surely he had to be the most handsome guy, if his voice was anything to go by. Anyway, what did looks matter when we vibed so well?

He was strangely intrigued with me, this person who could go on and on about herself to a complete stranger. 'Do you talk to all your friends like this?' he asked. 'No, only to you,' I said. 'I have no other friends.' Then I realized how very true this fact had become in the last six months. I hadn't made any new friends, though finding them was the second point of my fourfold pathway. Even my old friends were totally forgotten unless I happened to bump into them somewhere. I was totally satisfied with my one and only new friend. I didn't need more. Since we never met, I did not see it as an involvement. It turned out to be my deepest one ever.

My former friends stopped calling when told them I was 'really busy' or 'really, really busy'. Some of them tried to reach me and always found the land line busy. Very few actually got me on the phone. I started saying that it was perhaps left off the hook by the cleaning lady. I did not want any outside realities to spoil this dream.

I feel comfortable with him, I confessed to myself. Perhaps because he never offered an opinion on anything unless asked, I liked him even more. His mellowness and flexibility had to be my reason for gravitating towards him, I concluded to my sister. 'If you had said this after having met him at least once, I would be more comfortable,' she said.

We planned a meeting the very next day. 'Let's meet,' I said. 'OK,' he replied, and we figured a date and time for dinner the following week. He was late. Terrible, I thought to myself, and phoned him in disappointment. I like it when a man is chivalrous enough to arrive on time. It shows his interest.

The phone call is what saved this relationship, I always said later. We kept on talking and laughing about how he got delayed, until I suddenly found him standing next to my chair smiling down at me. I was truly stunned as I looked up at the face of the most handsome man I had ever met. My heart chakra spun like a top gone out of control.

He had huge brown eyes. And a long straight nose between well-defined cheekbones. I could press my entire pad of my finger into huge cleft on his chin. His high forehead led into to slightly curly hair, mostly black with a few strands of grey. His skin was mud brown with deep red glow at the temples. I went weak in the knees and was glad to have been seated earlier. Thank God I hadn't waited outside the restaurant.

His aura completely overshadowed his physical attributes. He radiated the most soothing and pleasant sensation, yet I felt a playful vibration attached to it, like a naughty child just about to get into mischief. I forgot he had kept me waiting for fifteen minutes before I dialled him and additional ten minutes before he arrived.

Earlier that evening, I had been on my way to the second point on my list of making new friends. That didn't happen either. After this dinner I just could not stop at friendship. I wanted marriage, and soon. I just couldn't wait to start a new life with him. My urgency for him shattered the fourfold pathway, even without his knowledge of it. His voice had gotten into my head and other body parts. When I saw him, I totally lost myself.

The dinner went off with a lot of laughs from him and many more stories from me. No sooner had we finished the meal and gotten into our respective cars, we were on the phone again. 'Would you like to come for a coffee to my place?' I asked.

'OK,' he agreed.

'Right now,' I said.

'OK,' he replied.

After that we spent most of the next six months on the bed in my new apartment. The apartment was a gift to myself when I decided to start living my life again. The bed became our lounge to watch movies, our massage parlour, our spaceship after a couple of joints, and our platform for raucous laughter and great sex. Sometimes it was the setting for a three-course meal of wine, khidchi and ice cream. At other times it was the battlefield to push and pull for our individual agendas while we each tried to keep our heads above the confusing rush of emotions. Lastly it was a bed where we fell asleep too exhausted from the above activities to explore anything else. Our fit was as if it was made to order, from head to toe.

The hormones just flew. Our conversations on the phone increased to five and six hours daily. We met every day after that first dinner. When we found the time for sleep and work, I don't know. Somehow all was well.

It was weird, the feelings that he managed to arouse within me. In no time at all he became my complete confidante. He was the only man in this world who inspired me to be a woman in the true sense of the word. Only for him did I enjoy dressing up and being girly. I never wanted to cross the line and backslap him even in jest like I did with other men.

I was a woman from day one until the end of the relationship, but a horrible woman, if I am to be honest. I didn't have enough experience in that role. I gave him a demonstration of all the negative aspects of femininity.

I had no idea who I was or what love was. I often spoke with authority on relationships because I had had so many. He sometimes spoke about love. He knew what love was in a deeper sense of the word than I pretended to have. It was me, however, who announced 'I love you' first, and I continued to say it vehemently throughout the relationship.

To him I was a good friend, period. I still don't know if he ever felt any love even for the briefest moment.

The desire to be married was perhaps the only thing I managed to keep a secret from him. Somehow I always ended up telling him things I meant not to. Three weeks after the dinner at Under the Over, the battle had begun. Someone's gonna get hurt real bad, I predicted.

In fact he never said anything even close to loving me, ever. He was the best I had ever had in every aspect, and I attached myself to him very quickly. The attraction had started even before we met. The meeting just sealed it all in cling film. After somehow holding back for the short time, the revelation poured right out of my mouth. I said I wanted to be married to him and have a child together, a daughter. I was weak; I was needy. I was greedy, and I was desperately attached.

He thought it was a joke. We used to do a lot of that kind of funny, but not so funny stuff with each other. Kind of slapstick humour which later we could recall and laugh about. We laughed at things any outside observer would not find funny at all. With him I operated at the level of an eight-year-old for long periods of time and thoroughly enjoyed every moment. He provided that sunny, carefree childhood that I didn't experience when I was younger. I think God sent him to me just for this purpose. He was my favourite playmate.

I pushed for marriage on a daily basis for more than five months after this announcement. It got me nowhere with him. He just would not see me as more than a friend. Then I decided to give him an ultimatum. I had shared my thoughts of going to

Dubai during our earlier phone conversations. I thought a six-month stint in that city would get him to miss me. He would soon realize how much I meant to him, and he would come to find me with a ring in his pocket. Absence makes the heart grow fonder, I thought. I had all the answers.

But as it turns out, absence makes you seek comfort in the arms of someone else, and soon that is what happened. Now we spoke and fought on international phone calls, he for his freedom and I for the commitment. 'But why not?' was my favourite line. I started feeling rejected and decided to do a shock treatment to see for the very last time if he would melt or not. The worst realization of all was that I was doing to him what my ex-husband had done to me.

Feeling overconfident that I would not lose him, I did the worst thing that I have ever done in my life. I lied to him and said that I had gotten over him and was calling off both our friendship and our romance. He really believed me. Gosh, I must have been convincing. A few days later, he didn't call as I expected. When I could not bear to not hear him anymore, I placed a call. I decided to patch up and agree to let go of the marriage monster. That was the last call before he blocked me out. He had moved on, and he was so damn happy. I felt intensely jealous of his new girl. I felt like the smallest creature on this planet earth at that time.

On the rebound or to teach me a lesson, he went ahead and got engaged to someone he didn't know at all in the one week that I didn't call him. He chirped away about his relationship. That was one of the few times he spoke and I was speechless.

After that I went into a depression deeper than the one that had hit me earlier. Everybody around me, including my sister, had thought I was doing so well, both professionally and personally. She was shocked and tried to help me out yet again. This time I was too far gone.

Professionally, Dubai had accepted me in no time at all. Now the six-month plan had to be made into a permanent arrangement. I deepened my focus on my work.

I could not imagine returning to Bombay and not seeing this man. I was sure I would land at his office, his house, anywhere, and beg him to take me as his anything. I longed for his voice, his touch, his smile, his laughter, his breath upon my ear, and his deep sigh as he settled deeper into the pillow. I wanted to be held by him, as sleep overcame me. I cried for nights on end. My eyes looked bloodshot. I stopped looking at myself. I hated myself.

I stared at his photographs from the digicam on the television screen for hours, just the few still pictures that I had managed to stealthily take when he wasn't looking. Tears poured shamelessly as I saw the smiling face through my haze.

It made things worse when astrologers said that his engagement would not last and he would return to me within three months. I kept a count of each day with hope and elation. I withdrew from my environment, waiting for his call. I kept my eye on the phone and imaged all the ways he would say that he did love me after all. Nothing came, no phone, no email, no SMS.

I called him and made a big deal about how he was doing the wrong thing and how his marriage would not last. He said he did not believe in astrologers' predictions. Then he blocked my calls. I had to agree to be shut out. Now all I had were the questions.

How could I have misjudged him? I wondered for the longest time. Did he know that girl from before? I kept thinking. How could he have been engaged in just the one week? Would it really work out being married to a stranger?

Having fought for various causes throughout my life, I somehow lost the fighting spirit now. I had never been the strong one when I was with him, and I could not recover.

I was now stuck in a whirlpool that had threatened to suck me under from the very first day I met him. Now that he had left I felt as if I was burning alone in a ring of fire that spread around this whirlpool now. I knew instinctively he was the only one who could magically lift me out, but would he ever come back? Could I emerge at all without him?

For the next three years that it took me to get over him I missed his one favourite phrase the most: so be it. It was always ready to insert it in any gap in our conversations. These three words convey everything so well. There really is nothing more to say or add on to them. Perhaps they served him as an easy way to end a telephone conversation without sounding rude, I thought later when he was married to another and I really missed my doctor's prescription of three times daily.

In Dubai I was isolated from my old Bombay life. My grief was like a sharp arrow shot into my heart. My speech was sparse and to the point. He had taken all my words and left me with just the phrase that I soon adopted as mine.

Getting over him was the hardest thing I have done in this life. Wherever I went, he did too. He just would not go away. When I looked in the mirror he was standing just behind me, smiling. In my car, I could see him sitting next to me, laughing while I felt the tears roll down.

When I visited the Eiffel Tower he was there supporting me as I leaned back to observe the entire structure in the frame of my camera. It was totally unreal. I used to see him in 3-D all the time. I was going crazy.

In Switzerland two years after the break up, I felt him slip his hand into mine as I stared at the awesome mountains and wished I had someone to share this moment. He never left my side.

When I threw a coin into the Trevi Fountain, I had a strange sense of déjà vu. I have been here before, I thought to myself, even though it was my first trip to Rome. I wished for him to be returned to me.

In New York, he sat in the seat next to me as I watched *Chitty Chitty Bang Bang* at Broadway in its entirety. I kept turning to him to share the moment. We really enjoyed that play. It is fit for eight-year-olds.

Why doesn't he just go away, I would think, and then immediately feel gratitude that he was there for me in spirit. I called him a few times from different locations around the globe that I trotted across. He used to answer the phone, not knowing it was me. We could hardly get to the how are you, fine, good, and take care. The lump in my throat didn't let the words flow. More than once my tears poured out as the line went dead.

I had to get help. There was not a single moment when I didn't feel his presence. I cried every night as I slept alone.

I started fresh in Dubai because he didn't call me back. Now I tried to blame him, but a little while later I argued on his behalf. Somehow, I could never see him in a negative light. Even his marriage to that lucky girl was somehow a mistake I had made, I convinced myself.

I made no friends at all even though Dubai is such a happening scene. I had only one topic I wanted to ruminate on, and even those closest to me did not know how deeply this had impacted me. No one ever figured this man meant so much to me. I had not told anyone about him when I was in Bombay, and now it was too late to start discussing it and trying to get in touch with my old friends again.

In desperation to help myself I sought past life regression therapy. My soul knew I would find him in one of my past lives. He appeared in five out of the nine lives I saw. Two of them had great significance to this life.

In Rome, I was Rosa. He was Lorenzo. I managed a bakery that my father owned. Every day, I stood behind the glass window and waited for Lorenzo to pass by with his friends. He turned back to look at me and smile before running off with his friends. He was seventeen. I was sixteen.

Trevi Fountain was just a short walk away from our bakery. I used to wish for him to marry me by throwing a coin over my shoulder into the fountain. One day he came to order a cake for his wedding. It was strange that he didn't even tell me that he was about to be wed while I served him Italian delicacies when my dad was not around. How could he just shock me like that? I thought. I went into depression.

I had wanted to tell him that I had feelings from him, but it would have been too forward to do so. Anyway I thought he knew that I loved him, because of the way he came into the shop alone, always eating and joking.

Seeing that past life made me realize why I had been so desperate to announcing my feelings to him in this life. My desperation to be married to him was clearer now.

I got deeper and deeper into methods of trying to clear my past karma. I didn't know where to start, and I sought everyone's assistance. I left no stone unturned in my quest to settle the bad karma I had created this present life by chasing him away.

I carried unresolved emotions from my previous life as Rosa. In confessing deep love to him, I had done what she regretted not doing. The strange thing is that I had felt love from his very first hello on the phone.

Slowly the reality hit me that he really had gone away for this lifetime, and it would be right to let him go and move on.

I did not want to move on at all. I was stuck. I asked God, 'How did I get into this mess?' He was silent.

In another life I saw my lover as a Brahmin girl in India. I was a man in that life who had fathered a girl child with her. She was sixteen as the Brahmin girl, and I was seventeen. After living with her for seven years without marriage, I abandoned her and our daughter and returned to my village. I lacked the courage to tell my dad that I had lived in sin. In those days a girl child was considered a curse, so I just walked away and left them alone. I had not been man enough in that life.

I married another girl of my dad's choosing, with whom I had many sons. This Brahmin girl had cursed me with the fate of being born a Brahmin girl in a future life and suffering the same problems she faced. Then she blocked me out from her memories of that life and all future lives as well.

I came out of this past life with an unbelievably deep understanding of our soul journey. I read many books after that. I got deeply involved in setting right the bad karma of all the lives that I had visited. Nine wasted lives is what I saw. I had to set things right in this lifetime.

I took on many assignments besides feeding cows and dogs. I fasted. I chanted mantras under my breath. I sincerely apologized to all the people with whom I had found past life issues. I know that sounds really weird, but I did it.

My ex-husband had been an enemy in one of my previous lives, and he had come to settle a score with me in this life. I apologized to him for my previous mistakes and requested that I be released from his karmic cycle. He laughed. I pray he does not return to me in a future life.

Being loving towards all is the core message that came to me. Let go of the excess baggage that you hold onto from various lives. Travel light. You have been here before and will again be. These are the messages that I got from the guides that wait for us after we are dead from the body and the soul is released. In the period between incarnations they help us to learn the lessons of life.

I found answers to some questions by the time I was thirty-eight. I still did not know who I am in this lifetime, but at least I had discovered that I had been confused in my previous lives as well. Maybe in my next life I will get a sense of the identity of all my lives combined. But for now I know what love is. It is a lesson learnt too well to forget.

I figured out indirectly why some things happened to me. After many attempts to resolve my past life karma with him, his beautiful memories still would not leave me. In fact it was worse now. I figured we will get it right in our next lives and I resigned myself to live this life with the lessons learnt so far.

Two years after we broke up, I got an appointment with a top hypnotherapist and blocked him from my memory. I had no option. Regression was the route necessary to my progression.

From that day onward I have never thought of him. The memories have just vanished. When I do think of him it is like a dream, and there are no feelings attached. I am a woman who feels no love, because I know only too well how much it hurt.

It is ironic that I blocked out the man who taught me to feel because I could not bear to feel for him anymore. He gave me my sanity. He could have cost me my sanity. This was a part of my life from thirty-four to thirty-seven.

We make the mistakes we make when we are hurt by one person and move into another relationship as an escape. Clinging and attachment are not nature's design. Love is an emotion to be given out freely to one and all. It cannot be demanded. In hurting ourselves and the other, we lose the opportunity for the most beautiful butterfly to stay with us. Love becomes a four-letter word.

We feel true love only once. It cannot be replaced by another. I will have to wait for another lifetime before this love comes back. I regret the day I was curious to read about another's imprisonment. Each day is like a life sentence to me because of that day I was so desperate to read the book.

I send a message out to the universe: I miss you so. Will his heart hear it? He had liked me just enough, but not enough. I want my moments with my best friend, lover, and soul mate back. I will be a good girl now, I promise. I pray for a miracle, as another long day ends.

Life does have its own plans and designs, and we mortals know nothing of the plans of the superior one. I learnt that in its true essence when I was thirty-nine.

———

I was at the crossroads again. The intelligent fourfold pathway returned.

Only this time I am trying to get over the very person because of whom I had the courage to completely let them all go.

I start yet again. In that order. Marriage for any reason other than love is not worth it. My love lies with another.

Forget the past.

Make new friends.

Start a new life.

Never get married again.

He did not know me from before when I first met him, and he had no idea what a lost soul I was. He was a new friend.

He won't know me now if he has to meet me again, and he will have no idea what a lost soul I am. He is the past.

CHAPTER 5:

Withdrawing

Hindsight granted me twenty-twenty vision. The mistakes I made in that relationship were so glaring as I looked back in regret, which is all I could do. What made me cling onto him? That behaviour was so unlike me. I felt even more regret for the things I did not do. I should have asked more questions. Now I had so many of them and no one to get the answers from.

I was even more confused this time around. I had loved him. In fact, I still did. I wanted him back desperately. I hoped he would return and wake me up from this bad dream.

I had been dumped again for another woman. This was unreal. Lightning does not strike the same place twice. I just could not get over it.

When I was strong, masculine, and responsible for everything, my husband left me behind. When I was gentle and feminine, I behaved badly and my lover left me.

Whatever I did, I was left for another woman. My identity crisis resurfaced worse than ever.

Had he always had the engagement plan? Was it a deliberate decision on his part to speak less frequently? Was I being seduced for the entire six months on the phone? Was I worthless? Was it? Was I? The questions stared at me everywhere. I had to get the answers or lose myself in this madness. I withdrew from life. Rollercoaster rides are not recommended for those with heart problems.

Did I wear a sign on my forehead that said 'Use me', like the trash cans in this glitzy city? Instantly I had the answer. He never used me, and that was the honest truth. He never made any moves at all. It had been me all along. I had invited trouble.

I secretly hoped it was a game that he was playing. I kept waiting for the day, as suggested by the astrologers, that he would return in the next three months. I imagined him calling me, laughing hysterically and saying that he really had fooled me this time. Of course he loved me deeply, and we would both be rolling with laughter in no time at all.

Ninety days and many cigarettes later, I was lost in the thoughts of what had been and what could be. I called him. It was final. The date was set. He was getting married in another three months. This was the last call he had taken not recognizing the number, and told me he was blocking me now for good. The line went dead as I repeated his pronouncement in disbelief. The picture of his return became dimmer and dimmer. Hope faded away, and a deep depression set in.

I was feeling weak and just could not get the inner lion to awaken again. This inability to pick myself up was new for me. I know that it is not the number of times you fall down that matters. It is the number of times you get up with enthusiasm that matters. I had no enthusiasm or desire to get up this time. I was tired and drained. I was wounded and feeling very battered emotionally. I wanted to give up.

I had used up my lifetime's energy supply in an effort to come out the winner. Now l just wanted to lose and sink into deep sleep until he came and woke me up. I could not do that either. I had to live only for my son now. It wasn't his fault, and kids should not suffer because of their parents handicaps. I had learnt that well.

I felt self-pity, followed by disgust. After a long time reality sank in. I started the actual process of accepting that I had to take care of the mess on my own. It took three full years to complete this cycle.

I had no friends now. I shunned new ones too. I had a deep desire to be left alone. I cut myself off from all around me.

I slowly started accepting that I had had my chance with true love and had messed it up for good. I accepted loneliness and looked inward, talking to myself because I had no one else I wanted to share with.

If only I had sat still earlier, I would have seen it, but I never had allowed myself to just be. I was always fluttering around and missing the real point. I kept pretending to the world that all was OK, when all I wanted to do was howl and howl and break down. I could never drop the mask, even to my nearest and dearest. If we wear a mask, we can't see outside clearly and others cannot see us as we are. They see the front we are putting up and accept us for that. Very few people understood me for the person I really was. Very rarely did the mask drop. No one was allowed to pass through the gates to know the real me as I was now.

People I worked with would get to see my old persona because that is what I could easily display to the professional world. It came naturally in the workplace. I looked smart, successful, dynamic, independent, and confident, totally the opposite of my inside state those days. I had many masks and was very adept at pulling out the right one at the right time. No one doubted my authenticity.

When anyone asked me out, I gave the excuse of having other plans. I tried to hide my vulnerability. I was hypersensitive to even the most normal situations. When well meaning colleagues suggested setting me up with a good friend of theirs, I resisted, as politely as possible. I was hurting very badly, but they perhaps thought my reactions were rude.

I masked my deep loneliness. 'I am alone out of choice. I am fine without a relationship. I've had my fill', I told myself, even though each relationship had left me feeling more and more unfulfilled. The last relationship, ironically, had made me feel good and complete without his even intending to do so. The end result had been the same. Now I had even less faith in men than before.

Strangely I was not able to relate to anyone like I could with him. Later I attributed this to the soul mate and past life connection.

The next two years went by in a haze, my head spinning, my eyes teary, my heart heavy. My footsteps dragged. My skin went pale. My muscles felt loose. My hair lost its shine. My bones ached. The lethargy would not let up. Desire to eat, drink, party, sleep, talk, or do anything had gone. Smoking was all I had left. This is an example of the kind of stupid things we do to sabotage our own happiness.

The first year after the breakup I was all alone. I stayed with my sister when I had first come to Dubai, but she was fed up with my smoking. It irritated her tonsils. I moved out, and we stopped talking. She wanted me to quit the habit that was my security blanket. I didn't care. It didn't matter. I wanted to be left alone anyway. No one would understand my grief. My sister knew that my ex-boyfriend was married now, but she never really figured out why I had come to Dubai and that I loved him so deeply. Only smoking could relieve me. It was more important than my family.

Those were my secrets now. She thought I had lost a friend when in reality I had lost my life. I could not imagine ever loving another. She thought I would soon be ready to see someone or that I was happy on my own. She had no clue about the depth of my feelings. I didn't want to share him and or anything about him with anyone.

Moreover, she thought of me as a strong woman image. It was difficult to drop this role I had played since childhood. I was too masculine to show my vulnerability and express my feelings. My grief was too personal. It felt like my funeral.

In fact, I was a woman only to him and to myself these days. Everyone else still saw my masculine qualities. It was just easier to pretend to be manly. Less emotionality is expected, and less drama takes place too. I also didn't want my sister to think of me as someone who had been dumped for another woman twice. I was not sure if I could handle that.

The real me was lost beneath layers cosmetics. The girlfriend who spoke about the mascara running behind the veils did not know I was one of those women behind my veiled windows and closed doors.

I even fooled myself for three years, until by mistake I happened to look into my own eyes. Then it hit me that my empty eyes didn't match my made up face. I masked because I was worried about more loss. It was an easy way to protect myself.

After a while the mask became a part of me. I could not let it go. I focused on my career and moved away from relationships for good. The career took me places, and instead of men I eventually turned to God. Three years later, I had begun a new journey without even realizing it.

First I had to face many twists and turns. There is no escaping the harsh realities of life. The web is so finely woven that sooner or later it traps us.

I was so alone and depressed, and now six months had passed. My old contacts from Bombay started asking me out. I met many of them for business, and I somehow managed to present my earlier identity. This part of my life was actually going very well.

These lonely men regarded me as a single woman. They knew that my son was away, and they tried to interest me in a concert or a drink or a desert drive. I always refused.

The hole was so big and so deep I would need the love of the entire planet to complete me. Because I had been out with so many men, I could truly appreciate my last love for what he was. Just the thought of going out with another man made me feel like I was cheating on him.

My friends soon gave up and moved on. I put them off with lies about how I was busy in the evenings, gymming or going out with friends from Bombay who were in town for the weekend.

I was actually glad when my phone went silent. I went silent for the first time too, and in that silence I found comfort. I had never before been calm enough to enjoy the bliss of no noise.

Too restless a soul, I often embarked on things first and thought later. I usually neared the completion of an event before thinking things through and figuring that I was perhaps doing the wrong thing. By then the project was almost done, so I completed it and jumped into the next one.

In the silence I got a clearer understanding. I would find a way out of the mess. I had found my way into it, and I would get out of it. I was trying to brainwash myself now, a year after the spilt.

My habit of rushing in had led me to change my name the first time around. Now I got curious and started studying numerology to become an expert on it. To my horror, I found I had been given a number that didn't match my date of birth. I was stuck. My life felt like a bad dream all over again. The only one way out of this was to change my name again.

I consulted leading numerologists, and finally I met one in Bombay who confirmed what I had come to suspect after studying numerology a year and a half. The number I had been given was destined to take its recipient up in life and drop me down when I was right at the top. Holy Cow! What had I done?

Things had looked up as soon as I changed my name the first time around. He had walked in. I was so happy, and no one knew what to attribute my happiness to. I thought it was him, but it had been the number that manifested such beautiful things in my life. Then when everything was perfect, it created chaos and removed all the good things it had given me, including him. That was a weird way of looking at it, but who said I was being very normal those days? Had I ever been normal? Numerology is powerful to those who believe, and those days I was ready to believe in anything other than myself. Later I figured that numerology does work, but it is only a small part of the entire spectrum that we need to get right in order to feel fulfilled.

During the next 'up' cycle, that number brought me increased financial success. Suddenly my affluence became a trap too. I had credit card bills piling up.

This is when I changed my name again. Overnight, the clouds lifted as I could not have imagined before. I got a salary increase and a double promotion, and I bought a new car and a house in Dubai. I found myself doing the right things at the right time. I was enjoying this, even though it all happened by chance. I sold my house in Bombay at peak rates, and I established my company.

Slowly, I became a more open, flexible person, less needy and controlling. What was I trying to hold onto anyway? The desert of Dubai had shown me that the tighter you hold the sand, the more it slips away. Sand remains on an open palm much longer than in a hand squeezed tight.

I let go. I was always at the right place at the right time anyway. The only thing I could not let go were my memories full of regret. They remained unwanted guests in the house of my mind.

Finally the tears dried up. Clinging creates misery for all concerned. He had released himself from this. I was still clinging to something that wasn't even there. I had to face myself and grow out of if I wanted to make progress.

It was a good lesson to have learnt, I could sometimes tell myself honestly, and great for my morality. I won't be able to fool around with anyone now. Feelings are to be respected, not played with. I knew now how it felt to be on the receiving end of a painful situation.

I had by now let go of the need to control also. I compared it to the earthen oil lamps we have in India. The part of the wick that burns is blackened and charred stiff. The part that is soaked in oil is soft and malleable. I had always been the burning part of the wick until I met him. Then I became the oil-soaked, soft part because of his love. I could not go back to burning, yet.

I figured out later that whenever I consciously look for something, I never find it. As soon as I truly let things go, they come to me. The magic happens when I let go from the bottom of my heart. That is what happened this time too.

I was quite comfortable with the depression now. I liked being on my own, and I actually enjoyed the silence. I had no need to communicate at all. I knew that this need would only come back if he was there. I accepted being silent at home for the rest of my life. There was enough noise at work. It was nice to come home to my empty apartment. The aquarium I had installed for reasons of feng shui also made a good listener on a really lonely day.

My new mantra was that it's as fine to feel bad as it is to feel good.

Silence now did not seem as bad as it had been a year ago, when I had first heard about the engagement. Then one weekend I felt like going out for a movie and realized I had no one to go out with. I started learning golf, the lonely man's game. My weekends were now taken care of.

Even though I was more deeply connected to my feelings these days and more inclined to be feminine in my thinking, I often chose stereotypically male activities. Some habits die hard. This is a good way to balance my masculine and feminine energies, I have learnt. When I think feminine, and act masculine, I have the best of both.

Amidst all of this, the astrologers, face readers, and others came back even more strongly. They called me when they visited Dubai, and I often met with them. Somehow I could never turn down these men.

I was travelling abroad too, quite regularly. I tried hard to embrace the new, but somehow he always landed up right next to me. It was as if he was enjoying doing this to me.

While planning my itinerary for a business trip, I spent as much time researching holy men in the region as I did arranging work meetings. I met at least one holy man in each country I visited. I gladly consulted others I came across in my travels, and I became acquainted with new things like acupuncture and aura reading. Such was the journey to find myself and locate solutions through others.

In Notre Dame, I felt like making a confession. I approached the priest and poured out my regrets without much shame but with many tears. I was attracted to a man who was married to another, and I really wanted him love me in return. Gently, the priest told me to love myself first so that receiving love from others becomes inconsequential. That is not possible, I told him. I hated myself. Pray to God, said the priest, and he will show you the way.

I kneeled and prayed and lit a candle. Tears poured down as I saw him reach out at the same time and light the candle beside the one I was lighting.

I was going mad. Every step and every effort to get out pulled me under. When would this be over? I had to be as still as a church mouse. I added the mantra of self-love to my list, but first I had to agree to let go of the feelings of love I saved only for him. Not a drop was available for me. I thought I might never experience that rush I had felt with him ever again. Wasn't it better to live with his memories than with nothing at all? I had to decide. Finally, three years after we first broke up, I accepted in my heart that it was over. I would block him out.

Past life theory says that his soul would come to meet mine when he was ready to forgive me at a soul level. It was obvious that he clearly wasn't ready in this lifetime, so I had to wait for the next life. Souls will find a way. I had to clear the old karma, and letting go was the only way to make a place for the new, even if that meant a new life, the next one.

With the help of hypnotherapy, I reluctantly blocked him. I learnt this lesson well and once and for all. He was meant to be the last one, and definitely he was not the least.

A few days later, I received a call from the boarding school. I maintained regular trips to see my son every six to eight weeks, and called him once a week as was permitted to all parents, but I was so deep in self-pity that I had overlooked things like keeping in touch with the school staff and updating myself on events. I was woken up rudely from my slumber and haze. Big changes were on the way. Lightning does strike the same place twice. This was the second time my son gave me a purpose to live.

Many of the workers at my son's school had gone on strike. The administration could not comply with their demands, and they threatened to protest indefinitely. All students had to be collected immediately. The strike came midterm, and all final exams were cancelled. I was scheduled to travel the next week as part of an important project that I could not delegate to another. I didn't know what to do.

I called my mom, and that is when I genuinely came to respect and love her as the woman who had always been there for me, unconditionally. It was only now that I recognized her for who she was. My inner stillness allowed me this realization.

My son and my mom stayed at my house in Bombay. At age sixty-two, she moved from her village to the big city to care for her grandson. I cannot imagine myself helping out anyone the way she stuck her neck out for me.

It was quite an unexpected turn of events. I enrolled my son in a good school in Bombay to finish out the academic year. He and my mother made an odd pair, but she took good care of him. He enjoyed his time at home after a long stint in boarding school. We kept in touch over the phone, and as soon as I returned from the business trip I went to Bombay. I saw my mom in a new light this time. Actually, she probably appeared as she always had, and perhaps my way of looking at her had changed.

My son had broken some kind of physical barrier with her. Now she reached out to awkwardly hug me and affectionately pat me on the cheek. He jumped all over me with the news that broke the boarding school – how the staff had refused to wash the children's clothes or clean the toilets and cook the food. Survival through those three days had been a big adventure for the kids, as their meals arrived from an army mess. They hadn't been forced to do a lot of their normal tasks, as the teachers and house matrons neglected student discipline in their rush to trying to manage without the help of the absent workers.

We tried to figure out how long we could carry on like this, with him in Bombay with my mom and me in Dubai. Mom offered to help for as long as I needed her to. I was amazed at this total support I received from her. Somehow I had always thought she did not care for me, or maybe I didn't know love and could not read it even when it was present. In fact, love was right around me all along.

Her philosophy of life was based on trust. Plant a seed and let it grow. Don't disrupt the soil every day to check its progress. That made a lot of sense now. She had planted her love into me almost four decades ago without the expectation that it be returned. For a long time, I had not reciprocated, but she kept doing what she assumed was her part of the deal.

Now finally, as a mom and as a woman who had been hurt, I could feel all her past pain. I saw her differently now. I silently thank God for choosing the best mom for me.

I see a glow on her face as opposed to the frowns she used to reserve for me. She found her peace. She too had faced tremendous pressures throughout her life. Living in a situation not of her choosing, she was always making the best of what she had. She had been searching also.

Now that I had let go of my resistance and my ego, I had found her love. It had always been there, but I hadn't known how to recognize it earlier.

After my son's exams were finished, mom had been helping out for more than three months. It was time to decide whether I wanted to send him to another boarding school or bring him to Dubai. I imagined his eyes lighting up in this beautiful city and how much fun we would have together. My old, impulsive self returned, and I decided to bring him over.

My mom was relieved that I had decided to spend time with my growing son. She was thankful that she could now return to her life of retirement, but that was not to be. I had to beg her to join me in Dubai, as I needed a backup when I travelled overseas. She agreed.

She has found herself, and she was able to help me to connect with myself. This time I allowed her to do that. I did not resist. She encouraged me to go to temples. At first I didn't want to, she was content to let me drive her there without me coming in myself.

The most crowded street in Dubai is the area around the temple. I had no choice but to double park as I waited for her. This went on for a couple of months, and every week it was the same routine. She never gave up on asking me to join her, but she never forced me either. Even when I found a parking spot I chose not to enter the temple.

Initially I sat in the car, air conditioning turned on as it almost always is in this part of the world, and I listened to music. I shut away the outside world and listened to sad songs about loss and longing. I observed what was going on in the world around me. Vendors sold flowers and other holy items on the crowded street that faced my parked car. I could feel the buzz of the scene though no sound entered my vehicle. People entered the temple with an agenda, all trying to please the gods, I thought to myself. Then a few weeks later, I observed a difference in the manner of the people going in and the expressions on their faces when they walked out. I rolled one window down just to hear what the buzz was all about. I heard only the everyday sounds. When I shut the window I immediately saw the electricity again. The sounds were preventing me from seeing the other things. I have to shut out the noise to see beyond, I thought to myself.

I kept the windows shut and continued to see the magic in people's faces as they went in and came out of the temple. Then

I noticed that all of them went in sad, and all of them came out happy. They all went in stressed and came out relieved.

The before and after pictures were striking. No sooner had I lowered the windows than I heard the afternoon prayer rise from the mosque nearby. At the same time I heard the temple sounds. The beautiful synchronicity of both Hindu and Muslim prayers made me feel strangely at one with myself. It took two religions to find one lost soul.

After that I always rolled the windows down. Let me overdose on music, I thought to myself. Next the sunroof came off. The sun washed my skin, and the music touched every nerve and fibre of my very being. I started secretly looking forward to these outings. I still said no when my mom asked me if I was going to join her. She described how nice it felt in the temple. I should go in just once and experience it, she cajoled. I listened closely now, but I didn't agree to step out of my car.

After a few more months of taking in the musical bonanza, the street sounds, the smell of flowers, and the altered expressions of the temple-goers, I felt curious enough to make an appearance. I decided to make it seem like a favour to my mom.

That day she didn't question me. Just when I had mentally agreed to attend, she had permanently given up on me. She climbed out of the car without looking for my usual no. I felt a physical pull to get out of the vehicle before it was too late. The car had become like a jail I had confined myself to, I later realized. I nearly ran after my mother. She had walked a few steps already, not expecting me. She turned around, and I saw her eyes well up with tears as I said, 'Wait for me.'

That jump out of the car was the quantum leap I needed to take before I could meet my higher self. It had to come from within. External forces can take a horse to water, but it has to drink for itself. There was no one more thirsty than I was at that time.

I am a regular at the temple now, two years since my first visit. All the holy men know me by name. I see energy radiate from everything there. I sometimes cry when I compare myself to how I was a few years ago. Other times I stand alone or sit and stare at everyone that walks in.

They come in tired and walk out confident to face the world. This place is like an energy refuelling station, and it costs nothing. The game I play now is determining at what point the expressions on their faces change. There is a threshold to cross before one can say one has entered the temple. It is actually a gate made by man to protect the gods from humanity. What a strange world this is. Doesn't God protect man from himself? How strange is it that man has to make a heavy gate to protect God from his creation?

Once you cross this threshold, there is no way you can hold onto negativity, stress, grief, or hopelessness. The presence of a stone statue turns everything to clay, and we are ready to be moulded into whatever he wants. We are truly transformed at that moment. I know when these people emerge into the outside world their energies will shift, but at least they know where to go to recharge again with no questions asked.

I love my mom for not giving up on me, her first born. I hope my son will say the same thing about me. I see the tiny acorn I planted in rich soil growing into a giant oak, and I know I am willing to just enjoy seeing him grow. My mother must have felt that way too, despite all the tug of war between us. A word of caution to the reader: don't go digging up your seed. Plant it and feed it and water it and talk to it lovingly and then just let it be. Trust that it will grow.

My dad may have helped me to find my masculine qualities, but my mom helped me to find myself in the man that I was pretending to be.

I now believe that life presents tragedies to help us find the closest and most genuine people in our lives. It is in times of real trouble that we figure out who our friends are. For the year that I moved away from my sister's house, she had no idea how deeply depressed I was. Because of our fight, I would not call her and talk about what I was going through. Like everyone else, she thought I was fine. Outwardly I was. I had no friends left in Bombay who would understand who I was now. They had a very different image of me. I wasn't sure I felt like telling them I had been left behind once again, so I made no contact with new or old friends.

When I invited mom to join us in Dubai, I was trying to say thank you, but did not know how. Around this time, my sister suggested that we all should try to live in the same apartment as a family. It was an odd family, but a family nonetheless: grandmother, mom, aunt, and grandson, son, and nephew all rolled into one. He was getting the love of three women. I thought I would also take care of the masculine side of things to let him enjoy that side of me too. What my sister didn't know then was that shocking news would arrive to all of us soon.

A few months later, when I was deep into past life regression, I discovered that my dad had incarnated as my son. No one was more shocked than me. My mom and my sister both agreed that they sensed a strange bond with him. Feeling close to other family members is natural, but this was something much more. My son's food preferences were identical to my dads, among many other similarities. This knowledge was a powerful message to me. Understanding that the same soul was back among those he loved changed the way I looked at everything in life.

Having been struck by lightning so many times, I had gotten used to big doses of anything. Good was finally coming our way, but we had had equally big doses of the bad.

This feeling of being loved unconditionally, first by my mom and now by my dad, was a gift from God. I felt like I had been magically lifted out of the circle of fire and provided with a bow and arrow to shoot this message of love to all.

Our loved ones come back to us in some form or another. Love makes the world going around. We move in groups as souls bonded to each other, preferably with love.

My dad had emphasized my masculine qualities to better take care of the women, all three of us. Now, when I felt like a girl within, he had come back as a young man to encourage and support us, and in fact bring us together as a family. It was unreal. My dad had been with us for the past twelve years, preventing me from really falling down or giving up.

For the first time in many years our family was complete, happy, and rich. We felt loved by one another. We did not shout now. We all had mellowed or grown up or been reborn with lessons learnt from the previous life. There was a desire to be together, and we could tolerate each others' foibles in a way that most families can't accomplish.

Love had overcome everything else. Finally we could all just be. My son brought everyone together, as if we were the same family of my childhood.

Sometimes you have to wait a lifetime to wear a Rolex, as my dad had, I imagine. Sometimes you get lucky enough to gift a Rolex in the same life, as I would for my son. 'The child is the father of man' took on a new dimension for me now.

When we returned from the Dehradun trip, my son spoke about his first love at school. I told him my story about love and loss, and I shared with him the lessons I learnt. I explained how giving birth to him had given me reason to lift myself out of the haze.

He asked if I didn't love his dad. I did, I said but that was in a different way. He nodded and said that he loved me anyway. Then he gave me the tightest hug I ever felt and promptly went back to his computer.

I also found in my son someone who could listen as well as my lost lover had. They weren't the same kind of conversations, but I shared my thoughts and events that had taken place during work or travel. I brought him gifts and stories, and most importantly I gave him unconditional love. We learnt to play golf together. We played squash together. We watched *Friends* together. We went to the malls and the desert and travelled on at least one holiday every year. We walked on fire. We laughed. We watched *Analyze This* and *Analyze That* many times over. We found common ground. After the talking was done, I learnt to listen too. I discovered he had a great sense of humour. He was my new funny man.

I experienced laughter, fun, childishness, love and peace. I was happy in the now, and I learnt to appreciate the moment. Fun is always available. We make life too serious. It's got to be lived in this moment. It is not about the previous moment or the next. It really is the now that defines our next moment. 'Enjoy the now' became the family mantra of all four of us under one roof

---

I thought a man could fill me up. I believed he was the missing piece. I chased him away while simultaneously chasing myself to the brink of insanity.

I am not the only person in the universe who has behaved this way. Every human being is capable of every experience and emotion. Most people would have probably done the same if they had been pushed to a similar breaking point.

The question is, How low are you willing to go to get the answers, even if it means getting sunk? Sometimes you must touch rock-bottom with your bare feet. How high can you let others fly with your findings? Do you take others with you in your ups and take care of them in their downs?

We are our own dragons as well as our own heroes, and we have to rescue ourselves from ourselves. If your ship doesn't come in, swim

out to it, my friend said some time back.

Spirituality did not just happen. I had to be willing to face the stormy sea to find that the waters helped me float. When I stopped struggling against the current, it took me along with its flow. Somehow I used the sorrow to transform myself. Eventually all paths lead home. I found myself on the right path without consciously placing myself there. Others are not responsible for our happiness. Even money and love are not enough. I trust that something bigger will come, and I'm not going to dig up that seed.

CHAPTER 6:

Thawing

I felt a source of warmth somewhere deep inside myself.

My withdrawal from life taught the beauty of silence, and that was my first step to reaching the core. I didn't know that then. I confused being alone with being lonely. I need not have been lonely, I realized now as I sat alone in the temple and absorbed every word from the priests. I had to catch up on the last thirty-eight years that I had been disconnected from God, but first I had to connect with myself, just as the father at Notre Dame had told me.

I felt like Superwoman. Truly humbled by the lessons of life, I was ready to dive into a cause I believed in. I was finally starting to thaw from within. The mission was to get this right. 'So be it. Thy will be done. Amen', I prayed silently and sincerely.

The journey I completed alone was the best trip of my life. For the first part of my religious journey, I only travelled inside myself, except for trips to the temple. It became my place to withdraw and to be silent.

No one realized that I was already on the path. I didn't know it myself until about a year later. It was a physical sense of comfort and radiating warmth in the pit of my stomach when I ascended the temple steps. Each time it was stronger, silently reassuring me that all was well. The seed was taking root.

I had been told to bow down and pray in front of our home altar from my earliest memories. I never did that, and I even stole money from it once. My mom and sister were firm believers. They prayed daily. I was a rebel and usually did not follow things that didn't come to me instinctively. Nobody explained it well either. They just said it was a good thing to do. I thought of it as something I was forced into from time to time, mostly during festivals. I really did not find any deeper or hidden meaning to it and therefore had stayed away.

Somehow I believed that praying was a girly thing, and I had been very busy enjoying myself as a boy. My gender-based excuse was inaccurate, and I knew it. Almost all the priests I had seen were male. I had seen all my cousins, boys and girls alike, pray to the gods every day before breakfast. That was the correct Hindu way. Some of my uncles and aunts would not even talk or say good morning until they had chanted the morning prayers.

Until now, I had never sought religion. This was a total shift from the inside. No one in my family even realized its intensity. Outwardly, all things remained the same, and my family knew that I was visiting the temple with my mom now. They didn't know I went there on my own. We were more loving towards each other and expressed it physically. Hugs were common. Mom said 'I love you' to her grandson every night as she kissed him, much to his annoyance. I teased him and told him to enjoy it, as she had never been physically expressive with my sister and I when we were younger. Better late than never, I sometimes teased her.

Sometimes you have to become a grandmother before you can understand that children should be loved with lots of hugs and smiles and encouragement. Pure discipline makes them rebel.

I was shy and embarrassed to discuss my religious feelings with my mom or my sister. I rationalized that they might ridicule me, but I knew it was just an excuse. I didn't want to go to them. I realized I needed guidance now, so I sought out the priests to answer my questions.

So basic was my religious knowledge, that I didn't know what to do when I entered the temple. Some traditions required visitors to cover their heads, but some thought it better not to, like the Temple of the Tooth Relic of the Buddha in Sri Lanka. The guide told me to remove the scarf from my head. It was very different from the gurudwara where they stopped me politely at the entrance and offered me a scarf to cover my bare head. I started carrying a scarf and watching others as they entered each different kind of temple. I wrapped my head if they did, or draped the garment around my neck if scarves were not required.

I wanted a deeper understanding and had many questions. I turned to the temple priests and found new friends in them. They were very unlike my previous friends.

I was usually the giver in all my friendships, but I found I had nothing to offer these people in return for the friendship I sought. They would grant me the wisdom of the ages, and I intended to greedily take it all in. Perhaps I could give back someday in terms of a big donation to show my appreciation to the temple. I was so naive.

Of course the priests asked for nothing in return. They were rather amused to see an adult with so little knowledge of even the basic customs, but they were even more amazed at the lengths I was willing to go for knowledge. I was a sponge.

They patiently taught me. Some of the rituals were really easy and some were tough. I performed them all. In my initial excitement, I overdid them. I started by chanting a certain Sanskrit sloka one hundred and eight times. This was the easy mantra that I started out with, and it took less than ten minutes to recite. I loved it so much I recited it at least thrice every day. A few days later another priest suggested I chant another mantra the same number of times at least once a day. I added that to the first one. Since I was already doing three rounds of the first one, I thought it only fair to chant three rounds of the second mantra too. Soon I was chanting more than six mantras, thrice daily. I laughed when I recalled my thrice daily conversations with my lover. I marvelled at how much I had changed in the last three years.

I thought chanting mantras was easy at first but my ritual became more complex as I took on more complicated mantras. Someone suggested it would be better to do sun worship and chant a certain mantra simultaneously. This involved waking up early to shower, facing the east, and pouring out water as an offering to the rising sun while reciting a mantra under my breath. I did it.

Then another priest suggested that I should eat only vegetarian meals on Tuesdays and Saturdays. It was easy to follow this diet at home with help from the cook, but sometimes at the work cafeteria I realized only after biting into a juicy chicken leg that it was a vegetarian day. My practice was not worth the amount of guilt I felt when I made a mistake. Keeping 'no non-veg' reminders on my mobile kept things straight. I punched in 2012 as I always did when the phone asked for an end date. I don't know why I chose that number. Maybe I would get a new phone then, or perhaps that was the year my habit would be set without a reminder. Later I discovered that many believe that the world is going to come to an end in 2012.

Then another priest suggested that I fast on Mondays, eating nothing in that twenty-four-hour period but one small meal that excluded salt, rice, and all other grains. I should also visit the Lord Shiva temple on Mondays and perform a ritual of pouring milk on the Shiv-ling. I started doing that.

Soon another priest suggested that I start praying a special mantra to Goddess Lakshmi on a Friday morning, sitting in the eastern part of my house and facing towards the west. I performed this ritual as well.

My phone was full of reminders. I had six mantras to be chanted one hundred and eight times each, three times daily. On Mondays I fasted and performed rites at the temple. I was a vegetarian on Tuesdays and Saturdays. On Fridays I prayed while seated in a particular spot. I made sun worship my first activity every day. Devotion kept me busy enough, and God sent my family to live with me in Dubai to doubly ensure that I had no time for anything else.

I did it all happily. I never missed hearing the car radio, a phone conversation, or anything else now. The peace I felt in that silence was greater than anything I have ever experienced.

These multiple chants reminded me of the time I wore eight rings and wouldn't let go of even one. Similarly, I didn't want to let go of even one mantra. The construction of a new metro system created long traffic jams in Dubai. I could usually do a few rounds of the mantras during the time I spent sitting in traffic on my way to and from meetings. While other drivers heard updates of the world news coming over their radios, I was in my own zone, oblivious to what happened around the globe. Air conditioning cooled the desert heat while my mantras thawed the inner regions I had frozen years ago.

The result was that I would arrive at the meetings absolutely calm and cool on the outside and totally peaceful and warm on the inside. My sense of humour was restored after many years. While my colleagues often complained of not finding a parking spot even when they reached the meeting venue on time; I, on the other hand was never delayed. I left the office early with the intention to chant mantras on the way, and I always found parking easily. This was the blessing I received from my dedicated prayers. The cosmos reserved parking spots for me almost every time.

Around the same time that I started chanting mantras, I decided to find someone to perform a pooja in my home for my son's birthday. We had done this religious ceremony every year until he went away to boarding school. I often missed that one small part of my married life. Now I wanted to behave like a traditional Indian woman, donning a sari and getting in the mood to pray and give thanks for my blessings. I had moved farther away from God after the divorce. Life had been too unsettled to perform that ritual even once a year.

I met an elderly priest with a long grey beard and sharp eyes. I think he saw that my request for the birthday pooja indicated a far deeper need to connect with and serve God. This ritual was just a step on the way to opening the doors of my house to him. I understood this after interacting with him during many other ceremonies in the next year or two. He saw in me a person who had grown from selfishness and superiority into the realization of hope and a higher power. He wanted to help me. He agreed to come over, and that began my first pooja in Dubai after having been in the city for more than four years.

After that there was no stopping me. Celebrating a pooja every month or two brought my family together in the most wonderful way. We bonded and the enjoyed the present. We felt the peace and well-being of our happiness together.

This started my journey into ritualism with immense faith that all would be well. I wanted my happiness to continue, and I truly wanted to find that elusive thing I missed. Somehow I had stumbled upon religion, and my conviction grew more and more certain that spirituality was the missing piece. I started believing for the first time that there is a power higher than myself and that this was the only way to seek his divine intervention.

I started believing that God would take care of me if I let go. I undertook multiple religious ceremonies and fasts to please the gods. I sought to make up for all those years that I had chosen to ignore him. I had believed that I had created all the good things in my life. Now I knew that nothing happens without his grace.

I later learnt that ritualism is not the only way to find him. We can sit in one secluded corner of our homes and be in touch with him. He is in us, not outside us. He is so deep within that we have to be really still and deeply connected to ourselves to encounter him.

The ritualism worked well for me at that time, and the figurines of the gods helped me to connect faster. My best friend, who has been meditating for years, says that one can find immense peace and feel the entire universe within themselves just by shutting the eyes and connecting with the breath. I hope to reach that stage soon, but for me this is the first step, especially since I came from a totally faithless perspective. For now I bow down before the growing number of statues in my altar at home.

It's strange how word gets out. I hadn't told anybody that I was getting more spiritual, but slowly the temple at home started expanding. Now I seemed to be a magnet to all those who wanted to gift me gods. They also suggested what mantra to pray to invoke a certain blessings. My aunt, who had always known me as a non-believer, took it upon herself to get me a prayer from her guru and an idol for my altar. I hadn't even told her that I was praying regularly now. I think it is an aura thing. We can sense energy from those who are tuned into similar frequencies. One by one I added to my altar. My rituals took up large parts of my mornings and evenings. It was like working two jobs.

Each member of my family was doing really well. Peace settled into all areas of our life. We did simple things like going to the movies, because we were all operating from and enjoying the present moment. Joking and laughter rang out through our house, even when there was nothing particularly funny. Even the rather timid housemaid chimed in. We had everything, and we appreciated everything we had.

I did feel that the family diminished the silence I had enjoyed. When I returned home from work, I encountered the television sounding at full volume as I walked back from work. That was a only a small thing, and later I learnt to find my inner peace even in the most noisy of places. I didn't know it then that one has to go really deep to find it. I started meditating.

Everything was going really well, and then it started going horribly wrong. My career had always been my strength, but now it was getting messy. I think I became something of a misfit in the corporate world, but I didn't see it in that way then. I saw some of my senior colleagues not delivering in certain key areas. I began to questioned things, first within myself, then with the head of the department. He listened and promised to look into it. When nothing happened even a year later, I got frustrated and wanted out.

Work was less inspiring for the first time in many, many years. Something was not right. I had originally taken this job as a six-month stint, thinking I would soon be called back to Bombay. The job had looked alright during the days of my depression, but now I was concerned with other things. My perspective had shifted.

After four and a half years in the same company, I saw big flaws which earlier I had not acknowledged seriously. Perhaps my new spirituality made me want to do more, but I didn't know where to start. Maybe this was God's way of opening a door for me – the door to the meaning of life, perhaps.

I was in the mood to quit, although uncertain of my next steps. I thought briefly of returning to India, but I decided I didn't want to. I loved Dubai. I saw the masterpiece that had been created in the desert, and wanted to stick around to see the progress of the city. I looked forward to travelling in the metro trains as I had done in Bombay.

Besides, this place rewarded hard workers well. I had experienced it first hand. When I started my life all over in Dubai, this city treated me so well. I had found everything here that I lost in India, including my loved ones, peace, success, and faith.

However, I thought it would be hard to do better than my career at a leading publishing house. I decided to take a short break to clear my head. Perhaps on holiday I would have a change of heart about continuing in the same organization.

This was around the same time when I decided to start life afresh; as the search through astrologers was over and was now replaced as a search through religion and a priest has suggested the symbolic washing off of the sins by taking a dip in the Ganges. This fitted in with my wanting to start afresh by going back to my birthplace.

All the threads were coming together now.

Life has taken me everywhere in search for that thing which was spirituality. It was hidden deep within and as each layer got removed it was a more and more feeling of finding it **_now_** that made this search go even faster.

We, my sister, my son and me took the most beautiful holiday of our lives in India last year. **This was the part of the religious journey where we actually travelled.**

We landed in Delhi from Dubai. Mom didn't come along, as she had visited this capitol city before. We settling into the hotel and agreed on the places we all would like to see. We started with a lot of historical monuments and soon ended up in temples. We had limited time before our flight to Dehradun, my birthplace. We had to prioritize our sightseeing, so we chose a wide range of temples spread across the city to ensure that each one of us got what we were looking for from this holiday.

I found a greater sense of identity with each step of the religious holiday in India. I experienced a steady, progressive clearing of the head. At each temple the message became clearer. A feeling inside me became more and more defined. I was realizing my higher purpose. Some things that had appealed to me all along were now not so attractive. Now I was not chasing success or money, but a sense of pride and fulfilment in what I did. Honesty and ethics were the top values I wanted to promote.

I was keen to set up a new way of working, some way to empower people. Most companies don't do that. They give their employees very little support. As I sorted out my identity, I gained clarity about what I would like to do.

I was looking for a wishing tree, and I found one in a temple just outside Delhi. Thousands of people come here and tie a red thread as they ask the tree to manifest their wishes. I did that too. I had a long, long list of wishes now. I had never prayed to God or asked for anything, and now that I accepted that he was all-powerful, I realized the silliness of my thinking that I could use up my entire wish quota at one go. It doesn't happen like that. Only three wishes were allowed. After much studying of my lengthy wish list, I ticked off three wishes. I used my wishes on behalf of my three dear ones. My intentions were manifested just a few days after our return from Delhi.

Tradition holds that if one of your wishes comes true, you are supposed to go back to the tree and remove the red thread as soon as possible. I was happy to do this.

Next we went to the beautiful Birla Temple in Delhi. I prayed to all the gods there and asked one of the priests to bless me with special aashirwad[8]. He smiled indulgently and gave me an extra flower garland from the altar. They sensed that I was a new convert and did not know that God blesses each one equally.

---

8 *few words of* **blessings.**

We visited my birthplace and the Ganges, which flows through both Haridwar and Rishikesh. I took a dip at Rishikesh. It was too crowded to enter the river at Haridwar, but we did a special prayer for my dad's departed soul at that site. This is something that most Brahmins do when someone in the family passes away. Until then, we had not performed any such ceremony for him.

Now suddenly we were getting so much knowledge and so many opportunities packed into one journey. Everything was facilitated with ease. Messages came to me even after the priests stopped explaining. It was as if my mind was released from all traps and I had started to understand the reason for my being. My purpose was to do something with my life, for a cause beyond myself. My entire life had been designed such that I would eventually realize that this was the only way to completion. The divine is within all of us. It is social conditioning that makes us seek things outside of ourselves. At birth, we are created as complete and perfect creatures. We lack nothing.

Ever since that day, I have been able to receive divine messages as though they are whispered directly into my ear. I heard the advice to stop asking for things for myself and think of how much I already have. I counted my blessings and thought of how I could give back to others.

I was beginning to feel a pure, white light from within. Its warmth was wonderful. I felt a total willingness to let go of each layer faster and faster now. I got the feeling I would soon find the gift.

The midlife crisis was resolved now, and my identity was becoming clearer. I was more certain of who I was. My parents had done the best that they knew and the best that they thought would serve my sister and I in the future. I could be myself now. I was true to me, and that is what matters above anything else.

It was time to let go of the boy–girl split. I had been fighting with myself, and there really had been no opponent all along. It takes two to start a fight. If we are one with ourselves, there can be no battle.

More messages came, including the message to start now. I understood that this was the right time in my life to spread the message. There are no coincidences. I had to live it and experience it to be convinced that there is no other way but through God. I had managed to be strong many times. I could be the anchor for those that might lose themselves in the maze. I could let them know the best way to get out of the mess is to go deeper into themselves.

It definitely was the time to get off the ride and be still. I had been forced by circumstances to be. Just be. What are circumstances if not a higher power forcing us to see reality? Isn't it something like laughing at a person who has only one leg until you fracture one of your own? Then the realization dawns about the pain of that situation. Isn't empathy something that comes only after having been in the same situation yourself?

I feel the pain of the universe. My best friend says the universe is within us. If we feel our own pain, we have it within ourselves to feel the pain of the universe. It is a question of priorities. If success, money, cars, and holidays are your priority, you are where I was just some time ago. It can take great personal tragedy or tremendous realization to get us on the right path to connecting with ourselves.

It is possible to live an entire lifetime without connecting with ourselves. Do you know anyone like that? I know me. I was like that. I believe in doing something worthwhile for others now. I am getting out of the personality that has trapped me until now. My own expectations of myself have changed. I am fine with falling down now. I don't mind all the scars or wounds or marks that I have gathered on my body and soul. They are my trophies of having lived life well. I want to live completely, and spirituality is the path to the missing link. I had to see the dark before I could see the light. I am ready to go to the next level.

I have to reach beyond myself and my family. It can be very difficult for my family and my closest friends to change the idea that they have of me. I have stopped arguing about it. The angels whispered to me that I have to reach beyond my dearest ones. The world is ready to be my family if I can take them as mine in my heart first.

All my chakras are working in sync. I don't need holy men and astrologers now. True prayers have the power to grant us a direct connection with the gods. Prayers are like the mobile number to the source. You can call the gods. They hear you. They are never out of network, ever.

Pain had eventually brought me to prayer. Prayer had brought me alive.

Some angels keep working around the clock to set everything in order for the big day when we will be forced to seek that elusive thing. Having a head start can make a difference. Be like the athlete who trains every day to win by a fraction of a second on the final day. Win for others. Be the angel that you were meant to be. Love, not fear, is the key. Love all. That is the message of the world's religions. Fear is the devil's tool to part you from the angelic being that you are meant to be.

The web of life had closed in on me and compelled me to go forward without any mask, lie, deceit, manipulation, games, or hidden agendas. I agreed. I had done all those things before and not enjoyed the outcome.

I am more gentle now, on most days. Sometimes, people confuse it with being meek. Those who are used to my pushy ways cannot believe the change and are wary. They perhaps think that this is a mask too, if they saw through my earlier personas.

The inner lion has awaked in a different manner this time. It is not leading the pack to find the next meal, but it is protecting the pack from self-destruction even if it has to go hungry once in a while. The soul needs nourishment, and it can survive on very little. The energy of soul food is abundantly available in the cosmos.

Hunt only when you must. If you hunt well on a particular day, be willing to let go of some of your hunger and share your meal with another who is less successful. This is my New Age lion philosophy.

I like my reflection now. I had to move alone to find my path in helping others. It is the survival of the fittest, and the fittest is one who anticipates and understands soul consequences even before taking action. Life is an observation, in that it allows one to stay away from the evils that may surround us.

When I looked inside, I was transported back to the no-man's-land that I had seen as a kid with my dad. It is pure, clean, and fresh, and it taught me not to litter my own interior, for it is the dwelling place of divinity.

My other big message came to me from my sister, who told me to ask the gods for direction when I exhausted my list of wishes visiting so many temples. I was really considering quitting my job at that time, but somehow did not have the courage to do it. I took a short break to consider my decision. A new job was one of the first items on my wish list. I made my last wish – to receive direction – at a saint's tomb.

Between the first and the last wish, I got my new job. All the directions opened up for me. Now I thought of the web of life in a positive light. Everything I did linking beautifully to the next thing. It was as if I had got hold of the right thread to unravel the knotted parts of my tapestry. I was unweaving the inharmonious designs and being given a chance to weave new patterns in their place.

My trip to all the holy shrines in India was the first time I truly accepted Hinduism and allowed the religion to wash and heal me. I returned from the holiday a new me. Something inexplicable had shifted.

I cannot describe the feeling, but events will show the connection. Even before we are born, God has planned every little detail of our path. Of course we have to do our bit, but our human plans overlap with the divine agenda. If we get onto the wrong track, he sends his angels to help us out and bring us back.

I had asked for everything on my list when I reached Fatehpur Sikri just outside of Agra on our way to see the Taj Mahal. Our driver mentioned that this particular Friday was a very auspicious time to visit the tomb of the saint. He said any wish could be manifested, and people came from all over the world to pray here. When I asked my sister how to proceed with all my wishes gone, she advised me to ask for direction.

I believe that he does not talk to us directly, but he sends his messages via the people around us. My angel turned out to be my sister. Her words made absolute sense. Tears pouring down my face as I touched walls of the tomb. I felt at peace.

I returned from this trip with absolute clarity and surety. Whatever happened, I would leave my job. The next steps I left up to God.

I resigned within a month. I could not wait to get out. I had no other job in hand. I did not even have a plan. I was sure something would come about, and it was the strongest gut feeling I have ever had about anything in my life.

Sure enough, I received a fantastic job offer within a week of resigning. An ex-boss recommended me to his business associate who was setting up a new venture. He was a respected name in the field, and I had heard good things about him. I took the offer. The new job was a start-up company in my area of expertise. It would allow me to apply my skills and knowledge to co-create something worthwhile.

However it was forty-five days of struggle. Everything was micromanaged. I knew I would never be able to establish anything, despite my best efforts, because I would never get a free hand.

I looked up at God and cried. This was the first time I had experienced such a bad run in my career. What was wrong with me?

My sister suggested it would be a good idea to start a company of my own. I resigned again. Angels speak through the people we trust. Again the angel had spoken. While completing the paperwork to establish my business, I realized what God had been doing all along.

He was systematically diminishing the mindset that drew me to work in a big organization. That is what I had always chosen to do. He made his first move by frustrating me so much that I opted out of the job that had doubled my salary in less than three years. Then he gave me the good job offer to first help me consider moving to a start-up company, which I wouldn't have done under any other circumstances. The offer had been too good to refuse, and it gave me what I needed. I believed I would be able to help set up a company with humane ethics. I soon realized that it would not happen here either. I began to think God had abandoned me, but that was not so. He was telling me to have complete faith in him.

I realized that God really was behind this when I started thinking of a name for my company. It had to be numerologically correct. I slept with the thought of working on the name the next day. I woke in the morning with a name flashing before my eyes: All Directions Media. I did the numerology for it, and my hair stood on end. It added up to the numbers **seven, eight, six**, in that order. My wish at Fatehpur Sikhri for direction was being manifested. God was letting me know that this was his gift to me and I should not ever doubt it. The word 'direction' corresponded to his number, and this was also the holy month of Ramadan. I went ahead and set up my company under that auspicious name from God. I consider it to be my special blessing from him.

This was the second time that Islam had helped me find myself. The first time occurred when I had heard the mosque prayers while waiting for my mom to return from the temple.

The second occasion was this where the only God who is also represented in a number came to me, a numerologically concerned person to let me know that faith in him is above all. Above all. My company was the best thing that ever happened to me, after the birth of my son.

I am so glad that I heard the angels through the sister and asked for direction. I am so glad that I was granted my direction. And it was through this career choice that I did find **everything.**

I formed the company with a lot of help from my sister both financially and emotionally. Then all the other doors opened for me. God had been testing me to see how much faith I had in him. Now my faith was strong. I believed that only he could guide me, and I had actually left it up to him to make me do the right thing.

I set up my company in a matter of days. It was really easy. I received marketing help from my ex-bosses and ex-colleagues. It was unbelievable. Overnight I was an entrepreneur. Angels surrounded me and looked out for me.

—

I saw the pattern now. Quitting my job, working for a start-up company and then starting up my own company all happened in quick succession of our returning from the religious trip to India. I had been granted even more than I had dared to wish for.

SO BE IT...

I realized God didn't want a monetary donation. He wanted me to donate myself, heart and soul. That was the only way to thank him. I had to give myself, and nothing less would do. And I did, willingly. I surrendered completely. The doors of heaven swung wide open then.

Even later, it struck me that he had got me out of a regular job and made me start my own company so that I would have the flexibility of doing my spiritual work in my own time. He opened up a new path for me so beautifully.

What can I say? The plan that he had in place is more perfect than anything I could fathom in my wildest dreams. I let myself be taken along with the tide in whichever direction he chooses.

It was a good plan. I trust the seed will grow a tiny little shoot any day now. It has taken firm root in the pit of my stomach.

I had been silently converted into a believer.

CHAPTER 7:

Emerging

We *will* die. Shouldn't we learn to live first?

I had awakened the deepest part of myself, and I felt life starting to flow through me. It was a feeling of warm tenderness opening my mellow side. I had never had these feelings for more than the briefest moments. Now it was all I was capable of being. My true persona had emerged.

I had embarked on this path very unconsciously. Everything else in my life been a conscious decision towards achieving a certain objective, except for the time I had fallen in love.

Yet the most beautiful part was realizing spirituality is the key, the most important link in the whole chain of events that line up as our life. Without spirituality nothing can ever complete us, and with spirituality we need nothing else to complete us.

The end result was to be complete in the simplest of ways, not through fame, glory, success, and other worldly trappings. It was the desire to be complete and to be at one with myself. It was my inner journey to set me free. I found

**the entire universe within me even better that the one that
I observed outside.**

Ironically, the more I sank into myself, the more I emerged.
When I totally drowned into myself and let go without fear, I
floated effortlessly.

The soul journeys through many, many lives in many different
bodies. Each life has its lessons to be learnt. Each lesson learnt
moves a soul ahead to learn the next lesson in another body.
This is how a soul evolves from life to life.

Sometimes we are good learners who accomplish more than
one lesson, and we are double promoted. We come back as
more evolved souls. At all times our souls look for a higher
purpose. The soul strives to find the reason for its being. Each
life has a definite purpose. Each life has a positive purpose.

The giant puzzle that is a life contains so many moments that
seem useless. We may think they are not beneficial, but that is
not true. Each moment in our life is a useful moment. Every
event is a learning opportunity, but we don't always see that
when emotions get in the way. Each one of us has a definite
purpose in the universal scheme of things. Nothing happens
without a reason, and if we use our reasoning ability, we will
do nothing unreasonable.

If a soul gets lost along the journey of life, we are given many,
many chances to come back to the right path. Angels talk to
us. What we classify as intuition is often the voice of our own
personal angel. If we pay heed we often avert disaster. If we
still do not listen, we are given many more chances to back out
of our plans. The universe steps in to prevent total disaster if
our plan could harm ourselves or others.

The universe has many different methods of intervention.
Our lives may change drastically for inexplicable reasons. We

may cry over it for years. We wonder why such and such a thing happened, and we consider ourselves cursed. When we are faced with the same situation years later, our emotions are cooler. We have learnt to see things differently. That is what happened to me the moment I emerged.

Emerging is an unconscious process. The chick does not plan when it will crack out of the eggshell. No one really knows when it will happen, but we find one day that it has pecked its way out.

One day, the shoot that had been planted within me emerged. Everyone could now see the tiny green tendril, metaphorically speaking. All instinctively knew I had been reborn.

No one saw when the seed was planted. Only I felt it. No one saw it taking root either, but as the shoot shot out, they all knew.

My friends, my family, and even strangers sensed there was something different about me now. I felt a sense of newness. I started feeling good and attracting positive energies from all around. I was ready to welcome anything into my life. This attitude actually got me everything that I had ever regretted losing in this life. I was back with a bang. The need to change was stronger now. I saw the permanent benefits for all my future lives.

The messages continue to pop out as thoughts. They are too powerful for me to handle the very first time they come to me. A few days later they sink in easily. When I struggle to assign a deeper meaning, I get lost and end up thinking the messages are too fantastic. Letting go is the most important message of all. Meaning comes only when I release the message from my awareness.

I returned to my simpler days of simple lists. I checked off every point on my fourfold pathway. I had forgotten the past, made new friends, started a new life, and avoided marriage. My feeling of accomplishment was sweeter than any other success

I had tasted. Sometimes we do manage to get one hundred percent in life after all.

I studied the list to understand how I had achieved all my goals. Then I realized that the list had been simple and realistic. It is important to figure out exactly what constitutes our personal one hundred percent. A good list is made with a realistic comprehension of what we can and cannot handle. One hundred percent is possible when we choose goals we can achieve.

This does not mean making an easy list that excuses us from stretching ourselves. We should go for whatever we believe in, but with realistic expectations. We are human beings and are allowed to desire nice things. We should always believe in a higher power than ourselves that rewards consistent and sincere efforts. We are then worthy of receiving our wishes.

Sometimes the method of fulfilment differs from what we have in mind. The result may be more than what we ever dream of asking for, as happened with me.

Make your list and chase your one hundred percent. Each person's list is different, and the universe is abundant. It will bring you what you need and what you can handle at each step of the way.

Life does give us a hundred percent. Again and again.

Being at one with yourself can bring you whatever you desire. It is actually a state of nothingness. Want nothing. Feel gratitude for everything that you already have and compassion for those who lack. Act to alleviate the misery of those who suffer in silence, and be humble about your deeds. Then the universe will personally check off the items on your wish list.

Those of us with material wealth have an opportunity to evolve. Charity begins at home. The smallest amount of giving returns generous energy to the giver and makes spiritual progress for our next life or our current one.

We all know that we can't take riches with us after death. Yes, we can leave our children in the lap of luxury. They too have karma to fulfil. If we can teach them to share a small part of themselves, we are assisting them in their journey too.

Souls move in groups, as was very clear to me when I saw my dad come back to our family to fulfil whatever unresolved issues he may have left with us. Similarly, I drove my ex-lover away because I had an unresolved issue from our past life in Rome.

The universe is too smart for us to outsmart. In the end, we have to comply. Positive thinking always counts. Not even one percent negativity should be allowed. Even on a bad day, we must try to focus on the good points of our lives to attract more positive energy. It's tough, but not impossible. Easy things are usually not worth it in the long run. We should be willing to sacrifice immediate gain for long-term benefit. Be persistent. Practice makes us perfect.

Two months after I started my company, the universe gave me even more gifts. More and more doors opened, religious ones this time. I let the fresh air in.

I made some advances without any concerted effort. I became a vegetarian overnight and had stopped smoking some time back. Every part of me was truly clean now, including my thoughts, my aura, and my inner self.

I thanked the universe for these additional blessings. I was able to let go things I did not need, because I truly believed that the universe would easily bring me the most suitable outcome. The energies all around seemed to want me to enjoy the beautiful dance of life. Even though I did not need any further validation, I was granted even more in a moment of stunned silence and total awe.

Soon after I sold my house in Bombay I dialled my ex-lover's number from memory to bid him a final adieu. I had deleted the digits from my mobile, but they were permanently imprinted on my brain. Numbers have always been my thing.

He answered after one ring. After brief pleasantries, he told me he had been divorced for six months. The end of his marriage nearly coincided with my religious trip to India, but this was one thing I hadn't dared to wish for.

He hadn't intended to let me know about the divorce. My head started to spin at the strange timing. I was leaving India and had sold my house. He was single again. Was I losing the chance to have real love back in my life? Could this be the most horrible mistake of my life? There was only one thing I could do. I turned to God.

God told me to have faith and see what magic can do. I left it up to him. The future is for God to decide.

The present is mine, and it is a divine gift. My special blessings continue. I have my ex-lover back as my best friend, which is more than I ever expected to have in this lifetime. I was struck by lightning again.

I always said that the phone saved us on many occasions, and it was true this time too. We chat over Google now. He hasn't read to me for a long time, but he talks more these days, sometimes about spirituality. Talk about zoning in! He speaks and I try to listen more. With him, I find it difficult not to talk. I open up again, but with caution this time.

We are just friends – best ones. He patiently explains the love I feel for him as opposed to love of humanity. He encourages me to continue on my path. He is also searching and cannot commit to more than friendship. 'I cherish you dearly as a friend', is the best thing he has ever said to me.

I am starting again and getting it right this time around. We hurt one another the last time, but that is the past. We dwell in the now and don't really look towards tomorrow. We both have emerged from our respective sorrows.

We had to travel on different trains for a while, but our final destination seems to be along the same track. We now have spirituality in common. We travelled long distances independently, only to gravitate to the same spot. This sets me thinking that perhaps that is what happens to all of us.

The times of greatest suffering can help us to find our inner landscape and float effortlessly on the sea of life. When I went deeper without fear is when I emerged. What if we had no fear? I don't mean no fear in a dangerous or a life threatening situation and being fearless then, I mean on an average day if we were to lock up/freeze all our fears. The negative forces would cease to have a hold over us.

Instead of freezing fear, I had frozen love. Just the opposite.

I had frozen love in the deep freezer of myself for the longest time. Now I had thawed everything from my system and felt so much better and alive.

This time, I decided to freeze my fears literally in the refrigerator in my house. I sat and wrote a long list of all the fears that I have ever had and continue to have even on a very good day. I include in this list every little thing that has the power to hurt me or pull me down.

So, I make the long list and put my name and date and signature at the bottom. I read it again and add some more fears. And again. I have a long list now. I fold it neatly and put it in my plastic water bottle. I fill this bottle with water for the last time and shut the cap and place this bottle in the freezer. To be left there. Permanently. LET IT BE. Forget your fears. Frreeeezzzeee them.

A word of caution: Leave some space in the bottle for the water to expand as it freezes and opt for a plastic bottle, glass will shatter.

Now that fear is gone, find love to replace all the space that has been created by doing this exercise. Get around to doing things that you love. Things that your family loves. Things that you think others will love. Positive actions should fill your life.

When you run out of things to do, move to the next level and start writing about your good feelings and all the good things that you have done. Inspire yourself. Be the inspiration that you want others to be.

The more you pour out the more it sinks in to your soul. Allow love to take over and dominate everything in your life. Loving unconditionally will take you faster to the path of spirituality. When love turns to compassion you are there. Combine this with meditation or silent zone to find your inner self. It need not be idol worship or mantra chanting at all. I am coming to understand that better and have used that time for more real work in the world.

Get in touch with yourself and with others. For a good cause. We have done enough of partying and drinking and can take a break to see if moving into this side appeals to us. Check it out. You may never want to check out.

Love should be the only reason for doing anything worth doing in life. Not greed, hate or fear. Love for the job that we do. Love for the family that we have. Love for self. Love for others. Love is really above all. Nothing else. Only Love. It seems like a very clichéd line, but that is the truth. The universal truth. Once you have experienced it the doubt vanishes. Faith flows in.

Giving is the other side of the coin of love. They go hand in hand. It is the best way to keep a positive balance on the karmic wheel of life. Keep giving. As much as you can. As often as you can.

Don't trash anything. Find someone who has a need for it. And there are plenty who do. In some part of the world. When you google for personal info all the time, spend some time googling for those that can be helped by you. Even a positive thought will already make you feel better. More empowered. Nobody else can give you your power. It is yours. It always was. Take it back and keep it. Reach out. Right now. It is there, always within our reach. Even a blindfolded person can sense where the real power is. Inside. We know that, and yet there are times we allow fear to overrule this knowledge and make us behave weak and powerless.

Try to be like water. And flow. Just as water flows towards the lowest point, try to recall a time in your life when you were that low. And from that point try to empathize with another who is in that situation as you were when you were at that point. Move in closer to this feeling that you had then, and do to them as you would have liked someone to do to you at that point in time when the world had just closed in on you.

If your black clouds have been lifted thank your angels for helping you and become someone else's angel for that time. I got this message more than once and I have decided to go out and seek those that need me. How can I help is not the question. I know how. Who can I help is the question now. I get in touch with some of the local support groups to find out more and offer myself. That is what he had wanted all along, and now He had **made** me so fulfilled in every way, that the only way was to share it.

What use is all the money and success and fame and all the trappings if you do not give anything to those who may have silently been the support towards your success. No one is ever responsible for his success alone. Enjoy your moment and remember to share.

As we sow so shall we all reap. Let's go back to being more humble first. Then the rest will follow.

When my love returned, I learnt the lesson of accepting things as the universe offers them. He had always been my friend, and he had not swayed from that, but I had moved to the extreme. I was that kind of a person in those days. I was now willing to accept him as a friend. I should have listened to him years ago, but I was not willing to allow his opinion to spoil my dream. The unpleasantness that ensued eventually helped me see things differently.

It is so important to remain flexible instead of making ultimatums. Imposing our agendas upon others is a sure way of losing it all. I am a better person now. Some days I have the wisdom to look up at the skies and thank the higher powers for helping me learn so well.

It is in the losing that we find. The words are spelled across the clear blue sky with the white clouds.

At one point in my life I had thought that there was no purpose behind it. Now I see that a perfect design had been present all along. Of course I had many options in the plan, and could have suffered less and advanced on my pathway earlier.

My mom often says that morning comes whenever we choose to wake up. This was my awaking. Even though it happened rather late in life, I think it is still well in time. Even if it had come a minute before my death, mine would have been a life worth living. I am truly grateful that I have so many more years ahead to take the messages forward. Or do I, in these years before 2012, the year I set my mobile reminders to end?

I had to go no further than my past life therapy guru to find the answer. Indeed, 2012 is the year beyond which many people believe the world will change. It is a grave thought. What is going to happen? I cut off my thoughts as I realize I am allowing fear to come in. I shrug off the thought altogether. If the world had to end today, so be it. What could anyone do about it? If we all follow the path of love, rather than fear, all will be well.

There are so many souls around us who are lost or losing themselves. As souls who have either managed to find ourselves or keep our sanity, is it not our responsibility to help others in any way that we can? Others are looking at us to be their guiding light.

All that is required of us is to shine our light. We do not need to go and navigate for someone else. We wouldn't know how to handle their ship. When our lessons of life are learnt well, we start to shine from within, and then brightest of beams can be seen for the farthest distance. When we peel the onion to its lowest layer, then the pure white light shines forth.

We are all from the same source. We each have the same amount of light within us. Sometimes we get lucky and find the light of what we are meant to do without any struggle in our lives. That is rare and I personally believe that when things manifest with ease, it is a gift for something wonderful a soul has done in a previous life.

Nothing happens without a reason is the other lesson I learnt from losing my love. A huge chain of events leads up to every little thing that ever happens to anyone at any point in time. It was not a coincidence that I happened to be looking for a book the day I met him. I had stopped reading for a long, long time, when suddenly a review of my favourite author's new book sparked my desire to read. The colleague who sat next to me in the office heard me say this out loud, and he offered his friend's number. I dialled the digits and the rest is history. Was that a coincidence? I say no. That's my opinion, and I have many friends who agree with this theory.

It is all a big plan, but its unfolding is extremely flexible. A minute shift in the actions of anyone may shift the entire universe to a new and improved plan, if the action we put forth is a positive one.

If the action we put forth is a negative one, the cosmos knows it. God cannot endanger the lives of so many others for the selfishness of one soul. The plan exists for the betterment of all.

When there are floods and bombings, that is a plan too. It helps us face certain realities so that we will not want to allow them again. Sometimes our souls get desensitized to suffering, instead of becoming more sympathetic. We start turning a blind eye. Our soul loses its sheen, and we do not feel empathy for our neighbours' losses. Then one day someone neglects to have sympathy for us. The lesson hits home. There are no coincidences. We invite whatever comes our way. If good has come our way, it is because we have invited it, and if bad has arrived, then we may have done something to attract it.

It is not possible for humans to have survived on Earth with just our own labour and intelligence, as we like to sometimes believe. Those gifts were important in our evolution, but is that what makes the planet spin or the sun rise? An intelligence beyond our comprehension surrounds us each moment of our lives. Even the ant has come with a higher purpose.

Human beings plug into the universe at the exact moment they are supposed to. They get lit up by life, as if by magic. When their job is done, their light is extinguished in that role, and they die from this body. They are reincarnated depending on the way they played their role.

Sometimes we end up doing things mindlessly. Being mindful is also called awareness. In being aware, we consciously choose the best options in our limited time on the planet. It is important to tune in and make conscious choices. Instinct will tell us what needs to be done and when.

Sometimes nothing needs to be done, as was the case with my ex-lover when I was supposed to just be. I didn't tune in, and I was tuned out. Only when I tuned in did the universe tune in too.

Appreciate the now. Value what you have when you have it. You never know when it may be taken away from you. I have learnt these messages well.

Grab the thread of your tapestry and never let it go. Be willing to see the dissonance in your patterns. Be objective. Tackle your worst mistake first. When you have apologized to the person that you hurt the most, many of your other issues automatically get resolved too. The pattern changes and your tapestry of life gains beauty. Don't worry whether or not you will be forgiven. Just do your bit and let the other party do theirs. If they won't, that is OK. You clean your own backyard. Be responsible for your own actions as they affect your soul. You will be surprised by what you start to manifest. You will be amazed at how much lighter you begin to feel.

Operate from the knowledge that we are all a part of the original source. A tiny fragment lives within us. This source is what takes care of the whole universe. We can take care of our universe. We are not helpless, and we are not alone. Angels watch over each and every one of us. Our personal guardian angels look out for us. The more we tune in the more we are able to connect with them.

Forgiveness is important too. Forgive all the things that did not turn out the way you wanted them to. Failure is an important part of the learning process. Forgiveness of own mistakes is the first step in accepting ourselves. Set yourself free from your limiting beliefs. Once we accept ourselves as we are, things naturally come to us.

There is nothing wrong with us. We are perfect in every way. Those who make us feel imperfect are also humans suffering from their own feelings of lack. We took on their negativity.

Let love be the only energy that flows through you. Stop struggling against life. There is a plan. Trust it.

After all these insights and messages, I now receive questions, and sometimes their answers too.

One of them was: Can the Lion play? That would be the most beautiful day. No fighting, no hunting, no killing; just a lot of lion love. Like the masculine element learning to contain the female energy, like the balance of yin-yang.

A lot of us confuse spirituality with sombreness, but I have found a unique quality of playfulness that flows when we let go and start accepting that there is a larger plan. The reality sinks in that we are just playing parts in a story. Why do we get so attached to our roles? They are going to change soon anyway. Do your best, and don't try to be larger than life. This doesn't mean that spirituality is something to be taken lightly. Even the pathway to it requires a certain amount of seriousness and depth, but once the barriers are dropped and the first few steps are taken, we can understand the lighter side. While retaining all its benefits, we learn to laugh at life. The more we drop our excess baggage, the more opportunities life gives us to play.

There are no free lunches in life or what follows it. What you pay for is what you get. Good deeds and grace help us earn a better life the next time around.

We will all have to emerge sooner or later. I have yet to hear of a tortoise that did not come out from under its shell. The shell offers protecting from a lot of perils, but in the end a tortoise must stick its neck out to survive. So it is with us too, but we achieve this by going in deeper to ourselves and eventually emerging. In this zone we find peace, joy, and happiness. We don't look to be told we are looking nice. We know it already. An inner awareness shows in our eyes too. The battery never goes out.

———

What I experienced will not be identical to your own spiritual story. Each one of us has a unique relationship with the universe.

That is an essential step towards feeling at one with the universe. It is what it felt like holding on to your mother's hair as you slept and cuddled into her softest parts without a care in the world. You knew she was there. You can experience that oneness again.

Everything becomes a challenge to look forward to. The problems are challenges now. The need for isolation disappears. We connect and interact from the energies of love. We cannot go wrong when that is the starting point, the end, and every point in between.

No matter what anyone else might say, I know my being a woman counts for something.

We can die later. We are too busy living right now. Living right. Now.

CHAPTER 8:

Shining

I look up at the skies and ask why I feel so happy these days. I love every part of my life. I look nice; I feel nice; I am nice. It shines through with no effort on my part. When true emergence happens, it always shows.

Allowing things to happen to us is what ends up giving us the 'wow' feeling again and again. We don't allow things to happen to us. We want to make them happen. This blocks the energy flow from the universe to us. The universe has just one agenda in mind for us, and that is to allow us to experience abundance. The universe really does want us to do a-bun-dance. To wiggle our bums and dance to the beautiful melodies of life. Tune in... the rhythm will get you.

I immediately identified with the story a friend of mine narrated some time back. The musk deer lives in the Himalayas and goes about its entire life looking for the source of the musk that it constantly smells. The deer does not suspect that the musk lies within itself. We are all like that musk deer, and we are so lucky that we possess the intelligence to understand this and take it where we will. The power lies within us.

When I set out to break all boundaries, I did not imagine that they would all be internal limitations. Now I know. As the innermost layer of the onion is peeled off, a beautiful gem shines forth. It sparkles like the most brilliant diamond, with a light purer than innocence and brighter than the sun. The gem is now exposed to the rest of the world. That gem is you. The pressures of life were meant to refine you until you could do nothing but shine. All you have to do now is breathe the light and the love in and out of your lungs. People will come to you, pulled by your glow. Keep glowing as steadily as the lighthouse.

What you see outside is a reflection of what/who you are inside.

I had no idea what a lost soul I was until now. The hard lessons of life allow us to become like paperweights that help other souls remain spiritually, physically, and emotionally grounded. We have to get ourselves anchored first.

The strands of my life are many, but I wove all the moods, themes, and adventures into a unified fabric. The people closest to me have also grown by seeing my metamorphosis. My pain and my gain have encouraged their belief in a higher power and the inner world of each person. Telling my story has allowed others to share their own experiences, and they share their lessons with even more people, creating a beautiful cycle.

I choose to focus on the here and the now. I must attend as well as I can to whatever life presents me with. No astrologer can predict how long I will have this opportunity for life lessons.

I realize now that my name changes were attempts to find a quick fix for the mess I created. They worked at some level, but they did not have the power to sort anything out from the roots. For that I had to go to the source that lies deep within. Easy solutions are not the lasting ones, and external solutions are not the genuine ones. We find the good stuff after effortful work of our own.

After all the name changes, stone therapies, and feng shui exercises, I came to see these practices as helpful, but limited, tools. I also realized that I was trying to change my essence through the superficial label of my name. The things that truly define us lie within.

No astrologer was able to predict even one percent of the events of my life. The best they could give was a vague idea of my receiving something great or doing something wonderful. My real life exceeded the plot of even the best film, and I get to play the leading role in my own life. I truly went beyond my wildest dreams, simply by looking inside myself.

The awareness comes in that right from the beginning we are all the same, from the same source. Our ultimate aim is to be re-untied with the source, after our journey and lessons are done through the realization that it lies within us. That is what it had been trying to do. To get me to be. In the being, I became one with myself; and found the missing link to everything.

This was my power of one. The Source will do anything to get you to come to it. That is all it wants us to realize – 'You have me in you. You are a part of me. Come to me. I am not outside of you, I am within you. Be one with yourself and you will find me'.

The feeling of being one is the simple feeling of joy we get when we are attending to a task with complete focus. When we are totally involved in that activity. That feeling is what we are expected to try and achieve in every act that we undertake.

The feeling of being one when driving your car, and enjoying the drive and the view and the journey. The feeling of being one when we are listening to music, gardening, cooking, reading, working or whatever activity that we may be involved in.

As we become one with the activity, love gets sprinkled in large doses. Without our knowledge. Involvement makes the love grow.

Manifestation is the art of putting undivided attention into a good intention. When we do that abundance is created in the thing we focus on. Love will flow, if we just allow it to.

I look back at my life and see how I used to flutter from one activity to another. I always had a finger in everything, but nothing gave me complete satisfaction. I was not giving my full self to anything. My focus deepened as I matured, but love was still missing. I didn't have very much enjoyment in my life. It is only now, when I am completely absorbed in the moment, that I derive peace and joy from my activities. The juices flow.

Each little thing that we do has the capacity to give us great satisfaction. Nothing is boring when we go deep enough to truly participate from an inner level.

We are essentially travellers across the universe and over many lifetimes, so it is in our interest to equip ourselves with as much depth as we can. Wisdom will come in handy someday, and knowledge is never wasted. The subconscious mind stores the knowledge and memories accumulated over innumerable lives.

We also accumulate scores to settle. I learnt during my past life training that we attract both past life enemies and soulmates as our spouses. In that sense, marriages are made in heaven and scores are settled in the bedroom.

The things that manifest themselves in our lives are always for our highest good. I can look back and laugh now at some of the most terrible moments of my life. I am so grateful that they are over, but I also feel gratitude for the experience of life in its many hues. I would not have been able to advance if those learnings had not happened through those moments of despair.

My life is progressing smoothly now, even though I have given up control. I can finally be honest, first with myself and then to those around me; there are no games, no masks, and no lies. There is no need, no greed. There is no want, no lack, and no fear. Abundance is my only reality.

The name on this book is my birth name. I have gravitated towards my roots, and I am happy to be a Brahmin now, and a female. I am a vegetarian. I don't drink, I don't smoke, and all this comes from within.

In the end is the beginning. Human society has advanced so much, and yet there is a global shift towards the basics. More and more souls are finding themselves in true peace and harmony when closest to nature. If we are as nature meant it to be, then we find ourselves reaching our destination much faster and with no road blocks. That is the original plan and in it is perfection that we yet have to duplicate or better. I have heard of cancers getting cured through alternative medicine. If you believe, it manifests. It's an energy flow thing, where positive and loving energy goes that gets resolved, dissolved and thawed.

I touched rock-bottom with my bare feet, and I bounced back. On my way up, I grabbed hold of a few hands. They were not stubborn souls like I had been. They were genuinely lost, and they allowed me to temporarily guide them. Later, we shared the lessons that we all had learnt through our suffering. I hope we will be able to fly higher and pull some more people up with our newfound strength. What fun would it be to keep it to ourselves?

I want more and more company as I ascend. My ladder is very different from the corporate hierarchy that allows only one person to sit at the top. God allows all of us to reach the highest rung and use it for the good of all. I want to care for others who are down, even if it means risking my very being all over again. I trust that the divine plan is even better than what we can imagine. Don't doubt the plan. Just be. Just live. Just believe.

I no longer need to use the masculine aggression I developed in my childhood for survival. The soul knows no sex. It knows love and compassion. My soul has the strength of purpose and resolve that it draws directly from the source. It is a believing soul.

We come alone and go alone, and that is the undeniable truth of life. Why should we be afraid to find our way alone between the coming and the going? This question was a large component of my search. At one time I thought that worldly involvement was offered to us as a temptation, so that we could learn detachment. Now I understand that we have to live, play, learn, teach, give, care, share, take, unlearn, and understand things again and again to really absorb the lessons. Only then can we move to the next level.

We are not meant to be alone, and the universe pulls us back if we try to cut ourselves off from reality. I tried to go into isolation after breaking up with my lover. The labour strike at my son's boarding school was the universe's way of getting me involved in life again. I had confused nonattachment with isolation.

Can anyone weave a tapestry with just one thread? Similarly, the universe is weaving a tapestry too, and we are the threads. We've got to get entangled sometimes in the process. Nonattachment lets us eventually come apart to create a harmonious pattern that pleases the designer's eye. When the design is woven, we have to lovingly go our separate ways.

I recall a time when I asked God, 'How did I get into this mess?' Now I look up and say, 'How did I get so lucky?' I thank him profusely for his blessings. I ask him to use me for any purpose. He has given me the opportunity to learn amazing lessons just in time for my fortieth birthday. I think he may want me to start a new life in a big way now.

As one part of my life ends, it marks the beginning of another beautiful part that I look forward to. I donate myself for the higher good of all. I am happy to go forth in love, but the future is not ours to see.

We create our own reality. Even though the larger plan is taking care of everything silently in the background, we are allowed to play our roles as we wish. We can add our own flavour to our characters. As we breathe life into our characters, we inspire the audience to love us or hate us for the way in which we play our role. We get rewarded for a role well played, not with an Oscar but with another opportunity to play a leading role, perhaps, as we have already shown that we could do justice to what was given to us this time around.

This is also an important lesson I learnt. Do what you have to, when you have to, in the best way that you can to ensure the best for all concerned. Better roles will follow based on your performance in this one.

So much faith is entrusted in us when we are assigned a certain role to play. Should we not trust the one that trusts us that we do have the necessary talent to take us through the role. He will only give us that much which we can handle, never more. He will give us all that much which we deserve, never less.

When the only one I had felt true love for was returned to me, I remembered the saying: love is like a butterfly, set it free; if it comes back it is yours, and if it doesn't, it probably never was.

When the butterfly landed again, I was so tempted to ask for the old love to be returned, but what I got instead was friendship. Deep, meaningful, unconditional friendship. No commitment. No long-term promises. No words of love. Just a lot of comfort. And laughter. And sharing and joy. And a feeling of well-being.

I felt like asking for more for a brief moment, and then the lessons that I had learnt stopped me from digging it up. I simply trust that it will grow into whatever the larger plans find most suitable for the good of all concerned. If returning him to me was something that had happened even without my asking or wishing for it, do I need to worry about anything at all? This was a message for me in this life. Let go. Be patient. Keep detached from the result, just focus on the now.

He tests our resolve in every way. I am strong with the energy I draw from him.

I have come full circle. Back to what I was born as. That was the most optimal thing for me. It was not an accident that I was born a Brahmin girl. I had to take lessons in that form in this life. I tried everything to avoid it, and finally found everything when I accepted myself in that form, Brahmin girl. Who can argue with logic that brilliant? Words fail me. Thoughts do it. I am in awe of that super powerful force that allows us so much abundance if only we let it flow to us.

There are times we try to superimpose our plans onto the plans of the universe. This is how we are the ones that block the divine from flowing to us. We have learnt so much at school and through our education that we forget that there are lessons to be learnt beyond these too. Simple ones. The highest form of education is really the simplest kind. Love. Forgiveness. Sharing. Letting go.

More doors opened as I branched out into a new area of life coaching. Life continues as normal, but there is a definite zing to it now, which was missing earlier despite all the corporate glitz and glamour. My new company is what allowed me to find myself and everything else. I get back to finding more directions towards offering myself in better ways to serve those that might need me through this gift that I have been given by Allah.

I continue to work with my inner feelings and my inner world. There are lots of things in there that still need understanding, but that is part of life. I will learn more and grow more. That is the exciting part of life.

We all have been given strong hearts, and we must use them for the right purpose. Let the fight be for the right.

In the end is the beginning. I have learnt new lessons and unlearnt some that have finished serving their purpose.

The shoot will grow into a strong tree and has in itself the ability to provide shade to the weary traveller.

In the end, all the threads come together despite having travelled in different directions all along. They have to all join together as the tapestry is finished and prepared for display.

This book is a guided tour of my life so far. It is not a random collection of experiences and thoughts, but an exquisitely sculpted one.

I am learning to give love unconditionally, and I encounter more compassion every day.

HE MADE ME FEEL LOVE. SO BE IT.

May his blessings go with you...30th April 2009, Dubai

About the Author

The author, Latika Tripathi now goes by the name Purvi Beri is a sales professional whose career with leading publishing houses include The Times of India, India Abroad (a www.rediff.com publication, U.S.A.) and Gulf News. A career spanning more than eighteen years across India and Dubai with assignments across the world, she has founded her Media Representation company All Directions Media in the U.A.E.

Over a period of time she has strengthened her interest in holistic development and learning. She is a practitioner of Neuro-Linguistic Programming, Time Line Therapy ™, Hypnotherapy (recognized by the American Board of NLP, Association of NLP, The American Board of Hypnotherapy), Emotional Freedom Technique ™ and Reiki.

She also consults on Numerology, Feng-Shui and other practices based on the energy fields that surround us.

For more on the author or her company visit:

www.purviberi.com or *www.alldirectionsmedia.ae*

For more on the book visit: *www.sobeitthebook.com*